CANADIAN

CANADIAN POETRY NOW

CANADIAN POETRY NOW

20 POETS OF THE '80'S

EDITED BY KEN NORRIS

ANANSI

Toronto Buffalo London Sydney

Cover design: Laurel Angeloff

The publisher is grateful for the support of the Canada Council and the Ontario Arts Council towards the publication of this book.

The editor would like to extend his thanks to the Canada Council and to McGill University for giving him the time and support to complete this project. Conversations with Judith Fitzgerald, Peter O'Brien and Ruth Taylor also proved most helpful.

Manufactured in Canada for
HOUSE OF ANANSI PRESS LIMITED
35 Britain Street
Toronto, Ontario M5A 1R7

1 2 3 4 5 / 88 87 86 85 84

Canadian Cataloguing In Publication Data

Main entry under title:
Canadian poetry now

(House of Anansi poetry series ; HAP 44)
ISBN 0-88784-138-4

1. Canadian poetry (English) - 20th century.*
2. Poets, Canadian (English) - Bio-bibliography.*
I. Norris, Ken, 1951-   II. Series.

PS8293.C36 1984   C811'.54'08   C84-098218-6
PR9195.7.C36 1984

Contents

Introduction

In his book *Epigrams*, Louis Dudek observes that "We have a completely new Canadian literature every twenty years." Looking back over the progress of Modernism and Post-Modernism in Canadian poetry we see that this has truly been the case. The poets of the twenties, forties and sixties have each made their major contributions and forced the traditions of Canadian poetry to be periodically re-evaluated.

Without Smith, Scott and Klein (as well as others) advocating a "Modern verse" in the mid-twenties and early thirties, Canada would have taken much longer to see beyond the Victorian garden presided over by Carman and Roberts. Without the push, in the post-war period, of the Contact Press/Cerberus trio of Layton, Souster and Dudek, and the imaginative poems of James Reaney, Canadian poetry would have succumbed more completely to the atmosphere of academic convention that was so pervasive in English language poetry until the advent of the Beats. In the sixties our poets forced all the windows open, letting out their voices and letting in the world. The singular talents of poets such as Atwood, Newlove, Nichol and Ondaatje have revolutionized Canadian poetry. The Black Mountain influence has been and gone, but former *Tish* poets Bowering, Davey and Kearns continue to make important aesthetic and critical statements in their work. The shamanic chants of bill bissett and the associative textures and weavings of the work of Daphne Marlatt have opened poetic channels which our early Modernists could hardly have foreseen.

As with each succeeding generation of Canadian poets, the young poets of the sixties have grown older and become the new establishment. This anthology attempts to bring together the next wave. In her introduction to *The New Oxford Book of*

Canadian Verse, Margaret Atwood notes that "The seventies were the sixties until 1975," and this anthology takes that year as its point of departure. Most of the poets represented here published their first volumes at around that time or after. Almost all of the poets in this collection were born after 1945, nine of them being born after 1950.

In editing this selection there were a number of poets I would have liked to include on the strength of their work, but they "arrived" as poets in the late sixties or early seventies. Their work has been obscured by that of the poets who immediately preceded them and deserves separate treatment. Although many of them are represented in Atwood's *Oxford*, their work hasn't received much critical attention. An anthology might easily be compiled that would include the work of Peter Van Toorn, Paulette Jiles, Dale Zieroth, Susan Musgrave, Tom Wayman, Brian Fawcett, Barry McKinnon, Robert Bringhurst, Gail Fox, Andrew Suknaski, Richard Sommer, C.H. Gervais, Douglas Barbour, David Donnell, George Amabile, Gary Geddes and David McFadden, among others.

My concern in bringing together the present anthology is to focus attention specifically on the poets of the eighties, just now coming into their own. There are many poets of this generation writing at present, but the poets included seem the most obvious and accomplished. Their apprenticeship completed, they are now entering maturity. I am pleased that this group includes an equal number of men and women; with the poets of the eighties we have a generation, in fact, for which this is possible for the first time.

These poets continue to carry Canadian poetry forward. Singular talents, they are hard to restrict to a set of beliefs or truisms about poetry, but it is possible to see in their work some common features. In the writing of Christopher Dewdney and

Artie Gold (especially "Relativity of Spring") we find a con-
tinued interest in the kind of linguistic experimentation pio-
neered by some of the poets of the sixties; Dewdney and Gold
share some affinities with the American *LANGUAGE* writers,
although their work is as different from that group as it is from
one another's. Although many of the other poets steer clear of
the poem as a vehicle for linguistic experimentation, they are
aware of the principles of textuality.

A number of the poets included come from ethnic back-
grounds (Di Cicco, di Michele, Farkas, Filip, Gunnars) and they
freely explore their ethnicity. Although, in the wake of Frank
Davey's important essay "Surviving the Paraphrase," one
would be well advised to steer clear of thematic interpretations,
it would be impossible not to notice the recurrence of emigra-
tion and exile in the work included in this anthology, including
the work of those who were born in Canada.

Surrealistic effects are employed with facility by practically
all of the poets included, but as an element of atmosphere or as a
way of leaping to connections rather than as an ideology.
Similarly, they have their metaphysical moments without the
need to recall Smith or Dudek or Eliot. All of their work has
been affected by the feminist movement; something has clearly
changed in male-female relations and many of these poets try to
assess the shifts. The spirit of regionalism that made its presence
felt in the seventies has also clearly affected these poets; their
sense of place is often quite strong and evocative (especially
noticeable in Prairie poets Crozier and Reid). Finally, one might
point out that the exploration of the quotidian is a characteristic
of much of this writing. These poets pay attention to the facts,
conditions and issues of living. Even their subjective lyrics are
written in the light of their understanding of a relation to the
world.

Owing to limitations of space, I've been unable to present

longer works and have, in most cases, decided against using excerpts. As with the poets of the preceding generation, many of these poets have worked with the sequence or book-length poem. The interested reader is advised to seek out Borson's *Rain*, Lorna Crozier's and Patrick Lane's *No Longer Two People*, Dewdney's *Spring Trances in the Control Emerald Night* and *The Cenozoic Asylum*, di Michele's "Mimosa," Filip's *Hope's Half-Life*, Farkas' *Murders in the Welcome Cafe* and *From Here to Here*, Fitzgerald's "Past Cards" and *Beneath the Skin of Paradise*, Gunnars' numerous book-length sequences, Henderson's *Paracelsus* and *The Viridical Book of the Silent Planet*, my own *Report on the Second Half of the Twentieth Century*, and Reid's *Karst Means Stone*. In fact, some of the best work these poets have done has been in the form of the book-length or long poem.

In reading through the poems collected in this anthology, the reader will find the poets often asserting their present position and outlook. Erin Mouré opens her poem "Post-Modern Literature" by noting the distinguishing characteristics of such an art: "Less to insist upon, fewer/proofs." Roo Borson awakens us to "The wasted intricacy of each snowflake," while Pier Giorgio Di Cicco informs us that we are

> flying deeper
> into the century, love,
> the lies are old lies with more imagination;
> the future is a canoe.

Aware of their moment in time, these poets all offer their particular visions of the present and of our individual and collective prospects for the future.

Ken Norris
Jan. 22, 1984
Montreal

Acknowledgements

The editor is grateful to the poets themselves for permission to publish their copyrighted poems. Many of the poems in this anthology were first published in magazines; many have appeared in books by individual poets. Grateful acknowledgement is made to the following:

For Roo Borson to Quadrant Editions and the author; for Marilyn Bowering to Press Porcepic, General Publishing and the author; for Lorna Crozier to Turnstone Press, NeWest Press, Coteau Books and the author; for Barry Dempster to Guernica Editions, The Quarry Press and the author; for Christopher Dewdney: "The Drawing Out of Colour," "Grid Erectile," and "Coelacanth," from *Predators of the Adoration*, used by permission of The Canadian Publishers, McClelland and Stewart Limited, Toronto, all others courtesy of the author; for Pier Giorgio Di Cicco: "America," "Flying Deeper into the Century," and "Relationships," from *The Tough Romance* and *Flying Deeper into the Century*, used by permission of The Canadian Publishers, McClelland and Stewart Limited, Toronto, all others courtesy of the author; for Mary di Michele to Mosaic Press, Oberon Press and the author; for Don Domanski to House of Anansi Press and the author; for Endre Farkas to CrossCountry Press, The Muses' Company, *Rampike* and the author; for Raymond Filip to Pulp Press, Vehicule Press and the author; for Judith Fitzgerald to Coach House Press, Black Moss Press and the author; for Artie Gold to Delta Can, Talonbooks, Vehicule Press, *CrossCountry* and the author; for Kristjana Gunnars to House of Anansi Press, The Muses' Company and the author; for Brian Henderson to General Publishing and the author; for Diane Keating to Exile Editions and the author; for Erin Mouré to House of Anansi Press, Harbour Publishing, *Blue Buffalo* and the author; for Ken Norris to Guernica Editions, CrossCountry Press, The Muses' Company, Coach House Press and the author; for Monty Reid to Thistledown Press and the author; for Robyn Sarah to Villeneuve Publications, Fiddlehead Poetry Books, *The Antigonish Review* and the author; for Sharon Thesen to Coach House Press and the author.

Roo Borson

Abundance

The moon: hoof-print in ice.

Someone's shoes chewing an icy path.
The wasted intricacy of each snowflake.
A field without a man in it.
A rusted plow filling with snow.

Talk

The shops, the streets are full of old men
who can't think of a thing to say anymore.
Sometimes, looking at a girl, it
almost occurs to them, but they can't make it out,
they go pawing toward it through the fog.

The young men are still jostling shoulders
as they walk along, tussling at one another with words.
They're excited by talk, they can still see the danger.

The old women, thrifty with words,
haggling for oranges, their mouths
take bites out of the air. They know the value of oranges.
They had to learn everything
on their own.

The young women are the worst off, no one has bothered
to show them things.
You can see their minds on their faces,
they are like little lakes before a storm.
They don't know it's confusion that makes them sad.
It's lucky in a way though, because the young men take
a look of confusion for inscrutability, and this
excites them and makes them want to own
this face they don't understand,
something to be tinkered with at their leisure.

Flowers

The sunset, a huge flower, wilts on the horizon.
Robbed of perfume, a raw smell
wanders the hills, an embarrassing smell,
of nudity, of awkward hours on earth.
If a big man stands softly, his wide arms
gentled at his sides, women dissolve. It is the access
to easy violence that excites them.

The hills are knobbed with hay,
as if they were full of drawers about to be opened.
What could be inside but darkness?
The ground invisible, the toes feel the way,
bumping against unknown objects
like moths in a jar, like moths
stubbing themselves out on a lamp.

The women sit in their slips,
scattered upstairs through the houses
like silken buds.
They look in the mirror,
they wish they were other than they are.
Into a few of the rooms go a few of the men,
bringing their mushroomy smell.

The other men loll against the outsides of buildings,
looking up at the stars,
inconsequential.

One of them bends down to smell a flower.
There are holes in his face.

This Is The Last Night

Night drips tar into the grass.
Lamps fall onto the pond, making
accordions of light, but no sound
ever comes of that. Hills
are like the cool brows of dead soldiers;
they don't look back.
Trees are offered up out of the ground, helpless bouquets.
The light of each star comes hurtling,
but the earth never breaks, there's no way
to kill what you most want. All around
the small towns are lighting up or going dead,
whatever they do best, and the frogs begin creaking.
The soft flash of a fish
makes pilgrims of us. It takes so little.
It is the last night, the moon hails on the pond
with no sound, the canoe navigates
through ruins of trees. How am I to tell you
the only thing I know? On the bank
a wild violet opens. A small purple cavern
that no one walks out of.

October, Hanson's Field

Frost chains the pumpkins,
like planets run aground, or
buoys the dead hang onto,
their eyes lit in the loam.

No more flocks of birds
that blow like a woman's gown
from tree to tree.

Hanson's field is empty
except for the sound
of a few last things alive.

I look at the ground
as if it were one-way glass.
The dead can see me.

Past sunset they send up their shadows
to lean against the trees,
like holograms.

Jacaranda

Old earth, how she sulks,
dark spin-off
wielding wings and swords,
mountain ranges, centuries,
our eyes with their impurities.

Dusk. Planets like spilled mercury
and the stars exuding
loneliness, the old battle
for which there are no medals.

Often I look in that mirror
in which things happen over again.
Useless. Or I look
to the teasing water full of days
and clouds that drift like smoke,
and hours when the head sleeps,
an inn for strange guests. If only
we were easier creatures.

But the jacaranda reclines
like a wise thing,
stars crystallizing
beyond its dusky plumes.
Here in the amethyst air of early autumn,
the dryness a talisman,
the moon the egg of a luminous bird,
the jacaranda's wand-like branches
command each thing to be.

The jacaranda with its feathery leaves
blooms clusters of amethysts,
and its winged boxes
lilt toward the green plains bearing
an imploded formula
for jacarandas.

This is the endless catechism of beasts,
each a question and an answer,
on which time
in luminous drops
is raining down.

Just Before Dawn

At the hour just before dawn
the streetlamps enter their deep irony.

The air is damp with the submerged wildness
of October, the wind that would shatter
all the trees at once if no one were looking.

At the hour when the rodents have barely managed
to conceal themselves, the streets are dark and empty
as if no one were alive.

The wind crescendos in the trees again and again
in huge waves that would knock you over
if they were made of anything but air.

The wind makes the fallen leaves scramble.
The ground tries to pull everything into it,
calling without a sound.

A book fallen in the grass:
who knows how long it's lain there full of shadows,
shadows of men who did things, civilizations.
Wet with uncut crystals of dew.

The bright red mailbox on the corner
full of letters lying in the dark,
from the world to the world.

The Transparence of November

The orchestra of the dark tangled field.
The moon holds the first note.

Silver-grey the old barn leans a little,
just beginning to rise.

Since early autumn the poplars
have been racing one another
and are almost here.

Whatever small flowers
I may have mentioned in summer:
forget them.

Marilyn Bowering

Wishing Africa

There's never enough whiskey or rain
when the blood is thin and white,
but oh it was beautiful,
the wind delicate as Queen Anne's lace,
only wild with insects
breeding the sponge-green veldt,
and bands of white butterflies
slapping the acacia.
The women's bodies were variable as coral
and men carried snakes on staves.

It would do me no good
to go back,
I am threaded
with pale veins,
I am full with dying
and ordinary;
but oh if there was a way
of wishing Africa.

When there was planting,
when there was harvesting,
I was not far behind
those who first
opened the ground.
I stitched in seed,
I grew meat in the earth's blond side.
I did it all with little bloody stitches.
What red there was in me
I let out there.
The sun stayed forever
then was gone.

I am scented with virus,
I breed flowers for the ochre
my skin was.
There is no sex in it.
I am white as a geisha,
my roots indiscriminate
since my bones gave way.
It is a small, personal pruning
that keeps me.
I had a soul,
and remember how it hurt
to be greedy and eat.

The Journey of the Suicides

They come from far away.
Undertakers sign to them
from the grasses.

They descend towards white sleep,
detoured under a pale sun.
They touch the countryside in passing,
but do not touch the morning
or the young woman
who walks in the warm darkness of her house.
Spring water refreshes their hands,
and they spread them forgetful, indifferent
as judges.

They do not see the turned fields
or the young trees.
Their long shadows drift
and colour the sea.
They have forgotten an infinity
of burning flesh,
and cannot hear the wind on the lake
or the sigh of foam
under a bow.

Wolves run the hills,
leaving the woods to assassins;
but these travellers have received a pardon,
and pass freely among the ruins.

Russian Asylum

One of the difficulties is in being
alone, not one with anything or one,
not even a dog or witness.
One of the difficulties is in not being able to move,
or breathe or speak—
to do anything, that is.
One of the difficulties is that you are always
going under when they come; you are fogged and weathered
with lack of sleep.
One of *them* fits something in your vein—
your vein swallows it, questionless.

One of the women takes your lover away.
She is kind and
feeds you when you can't hold a spoon.

You're awake all through it, but it doesn't last long.
Be reassured, brother,
believe there is nothing serious, nothing in it.

They walk you along the sea,
they ask after your family. They offer food and when you
push it away, it's you who look foolish,
yes, you do. Your reasons do not pass outside your brain,
not from eyes to speech—
and even if they did, what good would that be?
You're alone, and they help it along
with something good for you—something
painless and sweet.
        Over the official's desk applications roll in;
there are lives, happy lives, and people behind them.
        You could have been any of them,
then.
Oh, it's harrowing this—going under, going down,
writing out love like this.

Part Winter

Snow has ruined us
for warmer work,
we need blood to keep going.
Paler than sky, dull rabbits quiver and lie still
in the fields, their skins part winter
part fright.
On the hill
a doe breaks cover,
two others
(two streaks of pink
accounting for the shots)
bruise against the bottom fence,
eyes almond and buttered.
Too many animals in the valley:
hawk at the rabbit's belly too soon.
We shelter in a ruin:
stairways spiral into walls,
yew trees and vines
splitting up debris.
Fox has left a bird at the door,
its carcass solid and pink,
its neck gnawed to a thread beneath
a hammer head, a honey eye.
Too many of us and animals in the valley.
We meet at the white where hill and sky meet,
and black birds gather in and storm.

And If I Turn

i.

It's a long time
since I tried to live
in this room
where I learned to love you.
There is still the same table,
the small items on the dresser,
the window open on the night,
and a heart beating in the shadows.

I believe that everything is as it was,
that I am at home here, that today was a perfect day—
but at the foot of the bed

someone told me
how she weeps
as she works
for pleasure.

ii.

Your naked body touches this cool granite table

and will soon—without a sound—
become a quiet, insatiable enemy.
In your memory was there a glimpse
of a glacier?

Remember what else there was,
and warm your lightened body in it.

Peter Rabbit Sex Poem

Once he has finished sleeping,
he touches her breasts.
She wears a french corset—
orange with black lace,
size 10, on sale at Lily's.

This doesn't fit
with the skull-face
hanging between the spruce tree
and her window.
That scent is richer by far, but different.
      He turns in his sleep,
his touch pushing the pain deeper—
it shrinks like a cocktail cube
while the lava flows through her.

Peter Rabbit is in the vegetable patch,
his appetite for carrots undiminished
over the last 20 years (the book tells her),
and Mr. McGaritty still wants
to mulch Peter's skull with his shovel.
      She twists on her bone spit in the bed,
thinking of Hollywood, of a bra with cutouts
for her nipples. It is due tomorrow—
      something to change things,
to make her want more
than for him to turn to her, more than just him:
to want more
and to feel it beginning
to burn its way through from the core.

Love Poem for Lin Fan

No bud is so delicate as your tongue tip.
The sun has stopped.
The moist rock breathes for you.
A murmuring of blood is in my ears, in the wind.
When you awake, mist covers you.
Down here, in the forest,
we are still.

My mind goes no further.

St. Augustine's Pear Tree

The pear tree drops its fruit—
yellow stones ripe as olives—

not a fall out of love,
but a ripened fruit,
over over over
into the world.

In each act is separateness,
not accident.

The wind knocks at the branches,
the link is broken.

Think of overbloomed poppies, thick as paint
in the dust,
or the pear tree white with drought;

or when the self takes its scissors out
and cuts the cord,

heading towards light,

and so, falling inwards,
is born.

Richard Gustin

Lorna Crozier

Morgain Le Fay

From your beard and eyes
I'll melt the ice
when I let you in my bed
but I'll also tell you
of my other lovers
       how they made me shiver
       as they stroked my back
       how they praised my breasts
       with tongues

When you feel secure
and fall asleep
I'll suck the magic
from between your legs
seal your eyelids
with water-clear stones
Although you'll call out
no one will hear
You must lie in wait

Sometimes I'll appear
in a changed form
a crow snapping its beak
above your eyes
or a lithe white hound
licking the crack of your ass
Perhaps I'll be a serpent
you must kiss
before I writhe into woman again

Seldom will I bring you joy
The ripples from my stones
will circle
long after I have let you go

The Weather

I want to wade in liquid heat,
submerge in the light
where all things are possible:
black birds turn iridescent,
finches flicker like candles
from green to green.
I want to believe in you.
I want your hands
to carry the sun to our bed.

Instead the cold follows us
like an old wrong we can't undo.
Christ, it's summer, we say,
thinking the word
will make it happen.

Even our faith in seasons
is misplaced. A hand moves across
a pencil drawing of the world
and smudges everything.

The Child Who Walks Backwards

My next-door neighbour tells me
her child runs into things.
Cupboard corners and doorknobs
have pounded their shapes
into his face. She says
he is bothered by dreams,
rises in sleep from his bed
to steal through the halls
and plummet like a wounded bird
down the flight of stairs.

This child who climbed my maple
with the sureness of a cat,
trips in his room, cracks
his skull on the bedpost,
smacks his cheeks on the floor.
When I ask about the burns
on the back of his knee,
his mother tells me
he walks backwards
into fireplace grates
or sits and stares at flames
while sparks burn stars in his skin.

Other children write their names
on the casts that hold
his small bones.
His mother tells me
he runs into things,
walks backwards,
breaks his leg
while she lies
sleeping.

Woman from the West Coast

The beautiful one   the woman
who wears long flowered skirts
that cling to her legs
as if the wind were water
tells me that what I call sage
is not.
> *It's witch's moss*
> *I grow it in my garden*
> *have for years.*

She is an expert. She's read
all the names in books
and uses herbs to make
her spells. In an almanac
she records shapes of the moon
times of tides and planting.

I have lived on the prairie
all my life   have rubbed
the silver-green of sage
into my skin   crushed the leaves
into my hair   laid them
on the eyelids of my lover.
I wonder what
she'll call the wind.

South Dakota Refuge

Go to Sand Lake, she says,
in November it's a platter
full of geese, your geese,
the Canadas come down with the snow,
feed on marsh grass
before their Southern flight.

Along the border of the refuge:
wind off the lake, grey fog settling
on the water, the stir of wings.
Men warm their hands on thermoses,
cigarettes burn the morning air.
Against the cars like young boys,
bored, waiting for the end of silence,
the guns lean.

Indigo

Three sounds beneath the mountain:
a stream over stones,
the clacking of looms,
the younger woman laughing.

She is sixty-five
and still an apprentice.
It may be years before
she takes the name of her teacher.
Or it may be tomorrow.
Her teacher is ninety.
Her hands know everything,
they move with the quickness
of wrens.

Outside the hut, the wind
has found a form to take.
It sways on the line,
long strips of bright
cotton. The evening settles
like a dove over the valley,
the looms are silent. One woman
stirs dye in a wooden vat.
The other carries cloth
to the mountain stream.

Every day the old one grows
in the other's eyes.
There is much to learn
and much to teach
here
where all things are:

the mountain,
the stream flowing from it,
two women at the centre,
all the blue of the world
flowing through their veins
into cloth
for those who live in cities
they have no need to see.

Consummation

The wind began the camouflage.
Through its teeth it sifted
fine topsoil over her body.
It blew seeds into her pores
but the season was fall—
the wrong time for a planting.

When snow smoothed the land
she lay silent and shrouded,
but in spring she could feel
the sun yellowing the snow
to sparkling noises
and tiny grass blades sprouted
from her skin.

In the summer
her hair blew from the mouths
of the crocus.
Her nails sharpened to the points
of Russian thistles.
Her eyes were sky and water.
No longer cold   no longer quiet
she was motion   she was prairie.

Fishing In Air

What he fishes for changes
as light changes on water.
Whitefish, pickerel, goldeye.
There is a space in his mind
where they die, a pier slippery with scales
where their eyes turn to slime.

His line is invisible.
He has forgotten what lure falls
endlessly through water.
It could be feathered or striped
or a silver curve that flashes
at the slightest flick of his wrist.

If he could send his eye out on a hook,
return it to its socket when he reels in the line,
he would do so. If he could use his heart for bait
then cut it from the fish within a fish.

There is something he has never caught.
Something that makes him stand here
every evening, casting, casting
and reeling in.

Every time he fishes he is different.
The water is different, the sky, the way
the tern hangs in the air or doesn't.
What he will catch is a minnow now,
slim and golden, growing to fill an emptiness
in a lake he's never seen before—
no road in or out.

Barry Dempster

Links

She plays the piano, her head
folded into her bosom like a flower.
He sits beside her, the edge of one
thigh pressed on the gathers of
her dress. Chopin in the air. Summer
night tinkling. The parlour heavy with warm thoughts.

There are lovely words in his mouth, his
cheeks stuffed with candy hearts. "Run away
with me into the forest, we'll live in a cabin,
sleep on pine boughs." His throat is tight,
the collar of his hard shirt like a lock.
Moon shines on the piano keys, turns into music.

She is so innocent, pale eyes closed, one
foot tapping discreetly. A wolf howls out
back. She thinks it romantic—the hot
fur, growls trembling out of the body, wet
white teeth dazzling like stars. He hears it too,
dreams of protecting her.

When they get up, she catches a glimpse of
herself in the mirror: tiny, wedding party pink,
waist slim enough for fingers. She brushes against
him, sends him into the night steaming.
There's a strip of light on the road—he rides his
horse as if it were time, pounding into the future.

When they're married, they both imagine babies.
My mother is born during dinner one night.
Then I'm there, wanting to be. I learned from
my grandfather how to beat time. They look at
me, then down at their baby, a sixty year old
woman with blue hair. Grandmother turns to dust.

I place their bones on the piano bench, link them
together like chains. Music fills the room. His leg
bone lies over her thigh, his fingers like sticks wrapped
around her waist. Picking my mother up, I leave,
down the same shining road, horse hooves mixed
with the howling of a piano.

The Birth of My Father

My grandmother was on a smoky train when she felt
the beginnings of regulated pain, and at the
station, being shuttled into a dark taxi, she
marvelled at the spasms and was told by the driver
the head was already through.

In the shadows of the back seat, my father slid
into the leather air, a strawberry face
                        and a shriek.

I think about this in the silence of clean beds and
ready hot water, and wonder if my father was
marked by it at all: a disrespect of time, darkness as
                        a comfort, a trust of
                            rear windows and panic.

Sometimes, in dreams, I imagine him struggling with the
ticking of a meter, working against the motion
                            of a car.
He grips the two windows, forcing himself down,
        breaking
through worn vinyl, his first breath soured by gasoline
                            and old cigars.

Now, when the years have been impatient with him and
his body's tattered and beginning to fold, I worry
when he phones taxis, offer to drive him myself.

Three Women

They've got her lying in a long
white room, in a bed that bends
at the neck. To her right:
a woman who's lost control of her
nerves; the one on her left:
half-dead, waiting for the other half
to catch on. Outside, the surface of
the grass slides by in the wind, everything
worthwhile is moving; the three women
as well: walking away from their stuffy
beds with every breath. When the one dies
(the half-dead one) we're afraid mother
will surrender like a boy at his first
sight of blood. But she takes it well, smiling
over at the corpse before they cart it away,
saying: such a face, a face like a dried-out
apple, so unconcerned. The two women continue,
their silence as arrogant as a disease.
One morning, sitting, the twitching woman
cries out, falls back, sprawled across the bed
as if she'd fallen from a tree. That leaves
my mother, empty beds at both elbows
like ghosts. She lies there and listens,
silence a necessity now. The sky leans
down, pressing on her chest, curious,
like a doctor. One day when we go
to visit, she's dead—her and the
bed: one quiet ache of white.

Hippies

The slurred boogie of Volkswagen
vans came to a stop in the field
across from our house. Tall, lanky
melodies spilled out onto the grass
with their guitars and wide-eyed women.
One girl had stars pinned on her ears.
Another wore flowers instead of brassiere.

I started wearing dirty denims
and a pair of my mother's beads.
I'd sit on the safe side of our hedge,
smoking tea leaves, hoping they'd think
I was cool, but they never made a move.

At night they built yellow mounds
of fire, singing Dylan songs,
rising up to my window,
whirling me around the room.
My mother began locking me in at night
like one of the valuables.

The police came on the third night,
busting up a chorus of "Rolling Stone."
They were gone, like ghosts,
before dawn, heading off to
the pink horizon.

And then somewhere, in a fresher field,
they settled in, prancing about like
elves, tempting another dreamy boy.

In my field, they left
the black circles of what once
was light and on one lone tree
they drew a figure of an angel
braiding daisies in the hair of God.

After Peckinpah

In the theatre, feet on
a sticky floor, the dark
like an aura of disbelief.

The movie's done. More
deaths on that clean white
screen than in most hospitals.

The credits move in
like a bulldozer. All the remorseless
names, tombstones to murdered

actors, translations of blood
into notoriety. What do we
feel? There is no applause.

The dead, like a wave of flesh, have
pushed us into ourselves. Full
of our own reactions. Red

bodies repeat in our eyes
like flashcube light. We see
the world under blood. Men drowning,

bodies in slow motion—lyrical
spatters, stick limbs
shuffling into view like shadows,

the flickering of giant predictions.
The dead flail in the air, in the
night, the streets crowded

with their falls, the syllables of
prayers and curses lingering near
their mouths, their rattles.

What do we feel? Nightmares,
hurricanes of blood, landslides of
bodies, all bigger than any one of us.

Mary Speaks to Jesus

You came from the east
like the sun. I was bending
over a well, pulling up a full
bucket, facing you, not knowing,
the light, your light, spilling
over my face. There was an
explosion in my belly, my bucket
splashing down into the well.

You sprang from me on a cold night.
Your tiny bloody body steamed as if
it had come from a fire and your
hot mouth melted the ice from my breasts.
The earth turned green again as you
grew. Things changed with you. My
milk dried, you never wept like other
babies. I'd lay you under the sky, half-
expecting you to turn into a bird,
half-wanting it.

Everyone recognized you as a child,
even though most would never admit.
They'd look at me, eyes cast down,
thoughts gleaming on the ground before
my feet. They thought you were an angel,
not trusting you, a pink little boy, too
alive to know so much about the deaths
inside of them. How you put shows on for
all those people, quiet dramas, head
tilted up to heaven, pudgy hands open,
palms up, as if you were balancing God.

Looking at you, I could see the future.
It was hard loving you,
seeing the scars on your feet before
you could even walk, stopping myself from
constantly wiping away blood.

Forgive me. When I heard you'd rolled away
the tombstone, I couldn't help wishing
you'd rolled it down into the city,
sun setting, caving in the crowds.

Seasons

1/ I claim there is trust, room
    enough in the heart for
    buds and corn, for cold trees
    and useless fields of frost.
    Your heart is small though, a
    drift of snow in the corner
    of a blurred backyard.
    Eyes, no matter what
    their colour, see the same.
    We both watch birds wheeling
    south, black shadows on
    the endless streets; are
    we willing to believe
    in shapes, in patterns?
    Lie down beside me, the
    sky is soft and empty now.
    If suddenly, a
    stray feather revolves
    upon your wrist, think
    of one heartbeat, how
    without you, who knows,
    it might fall forever.

2/ Perhaps trust is a
    pilgrimage to the
    bottom of your heart.
    Roots remain with trees in
    bitter frosts, like a pulse
    in an unconscious body.

Warm then, warm, no matter
when, there are birds connected
to the land through our eyes.
Birds falling to eternal
July, south of doubt, in spite
of tiny hearts that often
freeze, mid-flight, an icecube
poised before an open mouth.
Come, a drift of you,
a promise patient
in my frozen hands.
Our hearts ache, a tight prism
of fist and reflected light,
a field of snow beginning
to blossom in the sky.

3/ I admit there is doubt,
arteries cramped with cold,
dead crows in the stumpy
corn, useless shadows in
the shivering sky.
But too, there is a heart
huddled against a fence,
a heart south of life.
Imagine this, you
lying beside me, a
drift of wrist and pulse.
What, an angel
outlined in the snow?
Trust, I trust the shape of
you, the pattern of your
heart falling into my
soft and empty arms.

Christopher Dewdney

The Drawing Out of Colour

In the silent radar forest
iridescent scarabs bear coiled trilobites
in slow procession
                              up the meridian of symmetry.
A canopy of precision optical instruments
eidetically dissolves in the rain of sensorium.

The voice of cicada in this forest
is the long sustained note
of an indeterminate philosophy
in a court where the evidence
neither confirms nor denies
its testimony.

We are informed.

Motion within time's arena
is repealed here with the proceeds
of all our invisible centres.
Each act in the scene of its occurrence
etches an observation gallery
into the rich and mute loam
of the forest floor.

The forest translates itself
into each perception generated
by the meeting of heaven and earth.
At twilight the bat's synaptic flight
darkly traces the foliage processional
while the leaves
                      cast in water
become as violins or cryptogam.
                                Witness

the drawing out of colour.

Grid Erectile

Because of its erotic & cool underparts & the sunset
    emblazoned on its membranous back. Its electric litheness.
Because it is a living precipitate of twilight.
Because it is large & soft with external gills.
Because it is tropical and changes colours.
Because the pattern on its back is a thin point.
Because they are so numerous and docile.
Because it whispers through foliage. An animate mobile tendril
    of chlorophyll.
Because it is like an adder, spawning mythology.
Because it is beautiful like a sleek girl with a choker.
For the milk sliding couples beaded with honey.
Because it is large and primitive & therefore closer to the
    dinosaurs.
Because they are the only lizards we have.
Because they fly around mercury vapour lamps at night &
    alight on suburban screens with their exotic & large bodies.
Because of their silent glittering black flight.
Because of a summer evening in 1954. It opened its wings &
    I received its revelation.
Because of summer nights behind the mosque.
Because it signals the height of summer.
Because of its mathematical precision at the infinite disposal of
    curiosity. Because its markings are the summation of
    military heraldry, the olive green of the English military.
Because it is a tropical species here in Southwestern Ontario.
Because they are nocturnal, tropical thin points of extreme
    beauty. Sculptural perfection in living and dense wood.
Because their chrysalis resembles a vase. Their humming flight
    & the insoluble intricacy of their June camouflage.

Because of the size & gothic modelling of their pincers, their
    chestnut brown elytra.
Because it is so tiny. (Weighs as much as a dime.)
Because it is pale underneath. Tawny above.
Because it is the eyes of night.
Because it is even larger, like a fox bat.
Because it is our largest and only cat.
Because they are capricious night gliders.
Because it is a predator.
Because of its inky fur. Tunnels twisting around roots.
Because it is a southern species migrating northwards.
    Evidence for an inter-glacial warming trend.
Because of their glowing eyes in the driveway at night.
    Their rasping marsupial cries.
Because of the caves.
Because of its unearthly face.
Because it is all of night.
Because it is a falcon.
Because it is sub-tropical.
Because it is a stilted & accurate blue mist.
Because it is the north, unwarranted in an ox-bow pond.
Because it is a tropical species slowly migrating north,
    starting at Point Pelee.
Because it is a sub-tropical iridescent metal.
Because it is the arctic migrating at the centre of blizzards.
Because they are astonishing aerialists.
Because the vacuum of space is so near.
Because of a dream.
Because they draw out the soul.
Anticipation. Electric gradients. The irresistible approach of
    the arc hammer. Excitation in the ion shadows.
Because they come after you & seem to float in dreams,
    the bend sinister.

Because of the storm.

Because of an erotic insularity in the moist almost tropical wind.

Because they illuminate everything in a grey powdery light and
turn the outside into a surreal theatre of marvellous intent.
The warmth allows the spectators to remove their clothes.

Lunacy & a saturnalian trance of corporeal clarity.

Because they are tropical.

Because they are both out of place & welcome.

Because they witnessed extinct races of fabulous creatures.

Because it is carnivorous & wet.

Because it is a carnivorous morning jewel in the sphagnum.

Because they are full lips & vulvas & are all of summer.

Because they are a tropical species here in Southwestern
Ontario.

Because it has huge leaves and is tropical with cerise jurassic
fruit.

Because it is fragrant & tropical.

Because its fruits are pungent.

Because the flowers are huge. Night glowing & perfumed.

Because of the pools.

Because their smooth mahogany pebbles are enclosed in
vegetable geodes.

Because of fovea centralis.

Because they flowered all of beneath into above and translated
it perfectly.

Because it is a living fossil.

Because of the colour & smoothness of its bark, the silence &
level loam floor of the beech forest.

Because of the fragrance of its gum.

Because of the wooden petals of their flowers.

Because of the waterfalls & the morning glen.

Because it is the memory capital of Canada.

Because I perceived an order there.

Because the concretions are there.
Because of mid-summer nights, memory steeped in fireflies.
Because it overlooks Lake Huron.
Because the cedar pools are nearby.
For it was once submerged.
Because it is a huge invisible river.
Because of the collections in grey powdery light of Toronto
    winter afternoons spent in the devonian era.
Because it is semi-tropical & on the same latitude as California.
Because it is a cathedral of limestone.
Because it is awesome.
Because chronology was commenced there.
Because of the black river formation. Last hold-out of the
    White Elm.
Because of the beech forest & what came after.
Because I got to know Lake Erie & glacial clay there.
Because I grew up beside them & they taught me everything I
    know.
Because it is a huge & silent underwater predator.
Because it is huge and primitive.
Because it cruises, hovering, long snouted crocodilian.
Because it is primitive.

Coelacanth

The existence of
an extinct species
is indicative
not of the circumstances
engendering its uncanny survival,
but the point at which
our nets coalesced
and forced his appearance.

This is not the place
of departure.
The event is invariably
prehistoric.
The five senses register
a vague roulette to it all.
A map
      with
      no
      corresponding
      geographical
      landmarks

From Book Three of
A Natural History of Southwestern Ontario

There is a language to predicate the adoration.

She is water, her essence an alarming grace unfolding past the edge of your control. Breeding miraculous witness. She is liquid darkness occult with desire. Command spillover. Trembling mica electron thunder. Distant blue spruce shimmer vaguely translucent pagodas rising like glass temples in the dusk. The ammonoid's gleam iridescent multi-coloured stage lights in a cretaceous theatre. Slow-motion trees augustean the clay bluffs, blue in the lake haze & at night the stars rain glittering onto the beach. Pyritized mother of pearl a refraction so ancient the dreams are blackened. This most devonian of raptures. A vowel away from the discrete crystals wherein her rude beauty gives way to angels. Soil the cumulative evidence of life processes, a recursive matrix & husky skin of utility stretched over the original rock. Limestone the accumulation of this evidence. As the planet turns into the photon irradiation of dawn. Our debit to the truth.

Beneath the lake a room. The water is electric. The smallest perturbation being transmitted through the whole undiminished. For its membrane is the precursor of the cellular envelope, budding cauldrons at the base of the falls. It is living. It whispers & moans & there are a thousand voices in the rapids. It is the medium of choice for internal predators.

Daylilies waxen cups of orange & red conspiring in the late afternoon sun. Dazzling cellular lattice. Rattlesnake point.

Dusty milkweeds at the side of the road. Summer cricket fields phasing a pointillistic audio plane. Waves of wind in the leaves transparent molasses. Insect voyeurs.

It is night and there is a yearning in the wind. Your heart a dusky corporeal fragrance streaming into the stars. And in the moonlight you can see the underwater trees. Devonian ocean floor commands the summer sky a fossil sea. Spicebush, Oak and Sassafras. The mouth of the Ausable. Blue evening dunes of the Pinery. The morning sun a coral resonance in the crowns of the trees. Leafless spring forest glowing tide against the sun fissured escarpment. Incremental heat of the vernal arc high over Collingwood.

Specific mist of August pink & gold. A morning light all day. The forest shade almost colloidal, darkening under the looming thunderheads. Lilacs. Nicotinia. A penetrating dampness, limp clothes & paper, the subway floors sweating under her sandals. Gracile her slim body. Gamelan the thrill of her hands. A proton decay cavern under the south shore of Erie. Her toes an almost Fibonacci sequence, her lips tasting of unknown cities. Rain shimmering in the Zildjian forest. A bat flying through Allen Gardens. Glass membrane ruptured into the June night sky, itself an infernal mosaic of irregular cobalt tiles, prismatic sparks at their interstices. Her sex flushed in the fire lithe under the trees. Words unable me to speak to you. There is a path for you hear if you see it. She was paradise renewed a tangible and immaculate dream. Blue the colour of opium in a dream once. As expensive as the sun reflected on blonde hair through tinted hotel glass.

I thought I heard the distant crying of a baby in the forest. Who would have abandoned so young a child this deeply in the woods?

This my Emissary

Sleep, come
unjoined with me.
I am radiant darkness,
a boundless prison
                    permeated with escape.
And what little the night recovers
is squandered at dawn.
For the heart has contrived a harm
borne of utter simplicity.

I have passed through the still eye of the storm.
I have seen the full moon in broken pine chiaroscuro
on the freshly fallen snow.
                    For the eye of the needle
is the still eye of the storm.
And when kneeling she wept
it was in the abject darkness
of total humiliation. This
my emissary
for the great silence.

                    In her misery we know it.

Winter Central

A spill contained in the fissure of light admitted by its own manifestation. An illumination of the crystalline moss in slanting light fissured by the lens of the control data truck. The surveillance car behind the control data van develops the angular momentum necessary for total magnetic silence. Quantized polarity of the federal asphalt.

The visitation of the luminous discharge is correct in the seething mass of frozen light waves already parting for the control blind. The figure, discernable only after computor enhancement, standing in the centre of the luminous discharge. The lens held by the hand carries filament waste-disposal sea of crystals, imperfect by the highway maintenance teams. Control data lateral response to the van maintaining radio silence in the absolute surveillance of the anterior vehicle. Astounded luminous figure holding the camera to the light-spill a fissure dump in the hot light of central winter. The image taken away by their heat, the image deflected by transmitted images from the bicameral care-package following closely. Visited by a luminous discharge of gases in the image clarification process. Wafer by-product of the programming, a non-actual event. Identity withheld for security reasons, as the negligible remnants of the countless passing fry the ice into a fissile brocade of tormented hydrogen

The Lateshow Diorama

Exploring the cold night of the lateshow diorama you come upon the outskirts of a small town, its boundary marked by an abandoned corrugated-steel hangar. The hangar is about a block long and sections of the roof are missing. The entire structure seems to consist only of girders & corrugated steel.

A guard dog, tethered at the far end of the hangar, barks. As you turn towards the first street lights the sound takes on a distant, rusty quality. The motion of turning produces an unexpected time dilation as the interior of the hangar is transposed into the back of your head a hollow glimpse of the stars & blue night sky through a tear in the ceiling. A gap to the stars as you turn now inpaginated a cascade of motion as you turn in pages of your tearing away from the image, the entrance, to explore the sleeping town.

As if you had left a trace, a phantom in time at which the olfactory dog continued to bark.

Pier Giorgio Di Cicco

America

The Tropic of Capricorn someone had
left on the seat beside me, somewhere between
Utica and Albany;

Miller going on about twats
about the pasting of billboards.

In and out of bus stops, nausea in my head,
the toilet smelling at the back;
the bus jolting on freeways; nightlights
rained on the window

the night I honeymooned with America. She took
me around like a sweetheart showing off her home town.
We came upon places where Miller had had her
before me. We stepped off at depots and she was friendly
with old drunks, with sailors.

When we passed apple trees gathering frost
her eyes softened; she seemed almost childlike.
And later, tall mills, saddening her landscape, the way
a woman thinks of years with a man she couldn't love.

When we passed train yards, she reminisced about
Miller in New York, nights they made love by the roar
of trains, sparks flying at the folds of her summer dress.

The night I saw her for the first time, I saw she
was a good whore—nothing to fall in love with—
fond of the young boys who'd grown with her; tall sons
of a sort who'd go on to elegize her, claim their
corruption by her, though

no man goes on to respectable wives
after her. She was nothing to sing about, the night
she lifted her dress for me.
But quietly   all over the world

her men return to their first nights with her.

Quietly, like small boys stealing apples under
furious stars,
they remember   with affection

the tough romance their hands build nothing without.

Flying Deeper Into The Century

Flying deeper into the century
is exhilarating, the faces of loved ones eaten out
slowly, the panhandles of flesh warding off
the air, the smiling plots. We are lucky to be mature,
in our prime, seeing more treaties, watching
T.V. get computerized. Death has no dominion.
It lives off the land. The glow over the hill, from
the test sites, at night, the whole block of neighbours
dying of cancer over the next thirty years. We are
suing the government for a drop of blood; flying deeper
into the century, love,
the lies are old lies with more imagination;
the future is a canoe. The three bears are ravenous, not content
with porridge. Flying deeper into the century,
my hands are prayers, hooks, streamers.
I cannot love grass, cameos or lungs.
The end of the century is a bedspread up to the eyes.
I want to be there, making ends meet.
I will not love you, with such malice at large.
Flying deeper into the century is beautiful, like
coming up for the third time, life flashing before us.
The major publishing event is the last poem of
all time. I am a lonely bastard. My brothers and sisters have
had sexual relations, and I am left with their mongrel sons
writing memoirs about the dead in Cambodia.
Flying deeper, I do not remember what I cared for, out
of respect. Oh *Time*, oh *Newsweek*, oh *Ladies' Home Journal*,
oh the last frontier, I am deeply touched.
The sun, an ignoramus, comes up.
I have this conversation with it. Glumly, glumly, deeper
I fly into the century, every feather of each wing
absolution, if only I were less than human, not angry
like a beaten thing.

Relationships

Everywhere they are talking about
relationships, though they hate the word,
though no one visibly vomits over it, and
everyone sneaks it into the conversation, using
the word for the sake of, you understand, convenience.
Everyone is talking about it. Primary, secondary
relationships, bad relationships, short-term
ones, long term, relationships that
couldn't work out, unhealthy relationships,
monogamous ones, a relationship lasting two or
three years, two or three minutes, a sexual
relationship, my favourite, phrase that is.
Relationships they work at, comfortable relationships,
the first big relationship, the relationship
I'm into now, the positive relationship, the
negative, a relationship based on understanding,
the relationship that's falling apart, the
strong relationship, the superficial relationship,
the relationship between two people, an honest
relationship, the mature relationship, the dead
relationship, the new relationship—though no
one likes the word, everyone uses it, all on
related ships, on ships with some
relations, relative ships, relating, shipping
some off to relatives, relishing tips on how
to have better relations.
                              Everywhere
they are talking relationships
and not having them, having them and not
liking them. Everywhere they are using

the dirty word. Relation ships us all off
to lonely places. In love—no one is in love;
they're working at the thing, committing, cementing,
forming attachments—it's all a bunch of
brickwork, constructing a sound relationship,
ironing out problems, breaking down barriers,
making a firm foundation, picking up the pieces
from a relationship. We are all frustrated masons.
Let's all build a good relationship and
crawl into it, let's all drag in ex-lovers
and bore each other to death, discussing it.
Let's discuss it and not do it, let's not and
say we did—let's be really careful about it so
a brick doesn't fall on our heads.

Let's look at a whole bunch of empty
rooms and discuss it;
let's get really old waiting
for a relationship that's right; let's
write more articles on relationships and
feel liberal, bohemian, enlightened.
Let's become the ministry of relationships,
the high priests of it, let's really get
down on our knees and bark at the moon,
meaning love, meaning the oval, heavy syllable
spilling out of our mouths and onto the
grass; let's wonder why sixteen-year-olds
are wary, conservative, going into law
instead of english. Let's wonder how long
before we're out there, pushing buttons,
not knowing other ways to say I love you,
wrapping up the foetus of fireballs.
When did we start discussing? What's this relationship—
this one-night stand with the earth?

The Poem Becomes Canadian

for Tom Wayman

The christmas poem for Tom
goes out into the snow, and remembers itself
sitting under large leaves,
and the landscape stirring with those things
it loved most
like a night full of stars
or those high rooms of sunlight where
cicadas imagine themselves drunk on their
own music.

The poem puts on a fedora, and dances
as old men will, happy with nothing but
mid-July.

The poem is lazy. it was brought up
under tuscan cypress, it has a heart
deep as the reach of an olive tree.
it does nothing better than to amble up and down
the streets of a small town, the dark cool of houses
wedged on the hot cobbles, the poem climbs the hill
towards the cathedral and lies under long pines
and whistles a little. the noon is everything to it.

This is why when the poem gets up in its sleep and
walks half-way to Vancouver or Windsor, or where ever it
is you are Tom, in mid-december,

I am a little surprised. It has come a long way
this poem. Like a simple handshake. At this moment

the poem will be happy forever.

The Explosion of Thimbles

You talk backwards and forwards through the dark,
to keep the arms going, to keep the brain rifling, to keep
love coming like oceans, like the need to be alive.

You talk mildly, and soberly (for a while), you talk
the leaves down, you talk mainly to keep the body an explosion,
one death-defying leap into the light.

This is the way I do it. One strong arm against another, a death
grip on another day, only to say love, to keep the eyes charged for
the april weather riding the wings of a bird. Only to see that,

you are pretending the world is yours, like always, one sure
mother against a world of thieves. You have to have

this one grow right, this child in you, this half-assed gesture of an
angel leaving the earth.

Beyond Labelling Me

I am so lucky, so ridiculously
lucky; luck oozes from my palm tree,
my fashionable view, sony tv,
lucky in luckiness, lucky in the hands
of the clock, I wheeze luckiness,
lucky in talent, lucky in friends,
lucky in Toronto, lucky to be in Canada, not
Zimbabwe, lucky in health, contacts,
money, I am so lucky—never did an honest
day's work in my life, never wept, never
depressed; I was born chipper, a happy-go-lucky
son of a bitch, never battered, always touched,
spoiled, lucky from the right side of the bed—
and of course absurdly lucky in love—
everything a gift horse. Things are exactly the
way they seem; I was born to the fashion, genes
programmed for sitting in the Courtyard Cafe, all my
books as good as printed as I think of them, poems
coming trippingly off the tongue, my fingers can
barely keep up. What is it to be alone. People appear
magically. What is immigration? What is feminism?
How do you spell rent cheque, suicide, debt. I know
you think I will live forever, so I will. I always
seemed less out at sea than you, because I was born
lucky, to show you up at parties; when you resist me
you will always know there were scores who couldn't.
I will dog you all the days of your life; when you get
close to the top you will always suspect I'll have
gotten there first. You will try to sleep with the
women I have loved. I will publish the story you thought

of writing just as you think you've caught up with
the lucky bugger. What can I do wrong, feeling this
lucky, for you. I can't hate you—it's part of my luck
and even that bothers you. I will always remain a
mystery to you. It sells books, and you will buy them
and understand nothing, and you will feel unlucky.

Ladies and Gentlemen, I present to you a lucky
bastard. If you go to sleep, I will be there when
you wake up, precisely as I was before—lucky.
I of course will have slept less, if at all. I will
have been up writing the poems you wanted to write, loving
the women you wanted, pulling off incredible stunts that
will bring me money, security, romance.

If only I could put my hands around your throat and
squeeze you like a lover. This poem can afford to be
cocky. It will appear blank to you. It is the way
you are—you see what you need to see.

Are you asleep now?
Is anybody there? Please wake up, so I can get
your goat first thing in the morning.
We go back a long way.

Jesus, how lucky can anyone be.
You will wake up and you will have missed me.
Another perfect day.
It must be hell for somebody.
Me? I slept fine. I have been around the world
for a long time
and I have landed in your heart, like a vulture,
sad, like a friend, like a lonely hunger
for the hours when you love me.

Mary di Michele

The Disgrace

But there's one disgrace we've never known:
we've never been women, we've never been nobodies
Cesare Pavese

A skinned rabbit sits in a bowl of blood.
In the foetal position, it dreams its own death.
I swell quietly by the warmth of the kitchen,
like the yolk that is the hidden sun of the egg.

The old wives and the new wives
are blabbering their gossip,
the intimate news of an idle moment.
Their children are blowing like seedclocks
in the yard. They are safe for now.
The girls are ready to be caught by the first
breeze and nestle in the grass.
Some of the boys will surely jump the fence.

On the first day I forget to play.
I am cramped in the corner like a snail
climbing the wall by the stove,
trying to sip camomile tea
with a blanket wrapped around my middle
to ease the first labour of blood.

My mother and aunts are eating
the unwritten stories of their lives
which they wipe away without a thought
and the crumbs on the table.

They all dine on the rabbit stew
together, good wives, good women, with an inch
of red wine in a glass and a carafe
brimming with secret desire.

This blood is anonymous and at times
gives off such a strong odour
that lettuce wilts in the hand,
and the new wine turns sour,
and onions cry in their sleeves.

My blood is knotted into worry beads.
Deliver me, if you can, from the cup
that I am, the spilling cup.

The ladies, *le signore*, are ready to tell their stories
as my mother serves coffee and cake.
When they crack the whip, out of their closet
mouths come dancing familiar skeletons:

uncle Gianni, who made his wife suffer, (poor saint),
bringing in his mistress to live with the family,
her own room, for the slut, and the wife to play
the servant; he sent the children to school
with extra money for lunch, such a treat,
when their mouths were so tightly shut
they could not open them to bite,

Maria Luisa, my father's youngest sister,
went mad in her sleep,
she tried to kill the elder, Chiarina,
with a knife, she cut her own throat
in a hospital a week later
and I'm named for her,
the consequences to be revealed by my stars,

while Giuliano was named in the spirit
of a good joke by my father
after a Sicilian bandit
hung on the day he was born;
my mother didn't laugh then, but she smiles now
as she tells the anecdote,
cutting another piece of cake,
pouring another cup of coffee,

Filomena, whose husband was sent to Ethiopia
to provide a repast for crocodiles;
she married his death,
then pined a long unrequited love for her own tragic dust,

and finally, of most recent interest, Anna's wedding night,
viewing for the first time the mysteries of a man's primordial
        appetite
for the blood he must claim as his own
and on the next day she had to study
the art of walking.

I am marking the day of my first bleeding
in red pencil in my work book.
I am ten years old.
Already they are plotting
a new and disquieting role for me.

Here is my initiation into the confessional of the kitchen
(will they stop my thinking?).
The men are in another room drinking grappa, smoking
        cigarettes,
while the hockey game minds its own business on the TV
        screen.

The men check the scores often, remembering their bets,
postulating the outcome of the series from a sophisticated
    knowledge
of the history and statistics of the league

Through the open doorway I can just see
a shadow school of the men's heads
bobbing like buoys in the white wash.
They think they are creating life in the living-room
while the dust of the outside world still clings to their shoes,
but even men, when they are common,
men of the trades: barber, plumber, electrician,
who make the real world because they lay
bricks for it, do not write their own histories.
They tell similar stories as the women
but with authority, with the weight of the fist
and the cry of the accordion.
However you will not read in books
the exploits of these family
men.

Patience on a Monument

The night is about the restlessness of women alone.
It's 3:59 a.m., the hour is ready to turn around.
Two women smoke each other's breath
sitting on a park bench, engaged in darkness,
thoughts glowing like fireflies
caught and cupped in white hands.

What about the man jogging in the nude around the green?
The cleft moon of his blue buttocks seems of no interest.
The soft voices of the women have been schooled
to mimic the stars of soap operas,
dressed in kitchen sink tragedy and universal values
acting on the premise of the perfectibility of men.

Sometimes we think too little and feel even less.
Sometimes we pause over the next line for over an hour.
The woman with a Greek heart steps into the role
of the statue of Sibelius
your basic igneous boulder with a hole for music
drilled into her heart.

A Fiction of Edvard Munch

More than death and death,
there is a malediction,
a pale green boy's sickness,
the way the organs start feeding on one another
when the body is starved for affection.

I can paint in the study the death of a sister
coughing blood into a porcelain, hand painted bowl.
When I paint this scene I paint the window into a corner of
the canvas,
I portray every detail of that corner, the ruddy, ruddy light,
every detail into the corner, I fill the canvas.
I paint the dark oak of the bed, the white sheets,
and a female face, my double, burning with fever,
a life already confined to the essence
of soft wax candles around a funeral bed.
She coughs into the bowl twelve summers and her thirteenth
winter
and no more.

So I paint the death of a sister,
so I draw the still life of objects,
furniture, rugs, drapes, woodpanels, a girl doll in a white
nightgown,
a clock on the mantel with the time fixed,
the affluence, the stubborn continuity of the material world
and a healthy income,
and the light, the light that translates all that
static show to the rhythm of music.

Walking the streets of Kristiana
I see the children of labour
crawl out of the slender darkness of mines
and into the tunnels of the street.
I do not know how to paint the darkness in darkness...yet...
how to paint black in black,
the details so few, a life nude,
a loaf of rye squeezed under a withered arm,
a pair of blue eyes, the wick still glowing,
in a coal encrusted face.

This I cannot paint so I go to the tavern
and talk about free love and unlocking all the doors of a
married woman's pleasure,
I can seduce, with my brush, a room;
it will surrender all of its vital parts,
but this woman that I meet so fatally,
makes me paint myself over and over,
as I paint the back she always has turned toward me,
and the head of buried gold I am forbidden to touch.

Finally, I realize that all details have to be erased.
Throw out the window, throw out the bed,
the canopies, the fragrant blue embroidery on a nightgown,
throw out the bowl and the pitcher,
throw out the serving woman holding them,
throw out the Good Book,
throw out the nick-nacks,
throw out all the god damned accoutrements of immortal
money
through which my family can avoid feeling directly any loss,
for what can be buried in rosewood and satin,
with the personal effects to be divided in lots among the poor
who are not afraid of disease.

Throw them all out and push the serving maid into my bed
to warm my numb, aristocratic toes, to jingle
the heart a little in the bank of the ribs.
I had to scrape my canvas clean
to begin again with a voluptuous death
posing naked on a bed.

Romance of the Cigarette

It was Sam Spade or Philip Marlowe
that made you famous
acquiring personality through
the ambience you emanate
of glamour and sex appeal
when fantasy outstrips
courage or The Act
as it often does.

Hanging there, erect in men's mouths,
you suggest the pyrotechnics of male sex
as the hero has no time to love,
he's too busy working on the next case.
It's only women who are fooled
into thinking sex more important,
they think they can get away with murder
when they invite good men into their beds.

But in American movies they wise up,
especially when Chandler writes the screenplay:
the heart's a chess game where the queen's lost
or the closest thing to death in life.

The Food of Love

White wine, fruity bouquet of chablis
is compatible with fish.
A poached eye, an opal,
witnesses how the candlelight conducts
with the batons of knife and fork,
deboning fish,
a solo flute,
all the cutlery of romance
we hunger for.

The woman tests her teeth
with her tongue,
a slim pink file
exposing in this gesture,
an invitation,
desire,
back bone of trout
picked clean
except for head and tail,
brain untouched,
a taste that's also ignorant
of delicacy in the cheek.

The problem of how to love intelligently
perplexes us,
carrying, as we do, the heart around
in a flight bag.

A voice singing from the past of failed love,
in such lines of jazz Sartre perceived
his only intimation of immortality.
Billie Holliday spinning on the stereo:
"He put me on a pedestal and then
he let me down,
he let me down..."
a needle conveying the feeling
in the fluted singing
of a voice like polished silver
gleaming from a heap of trash.

The Moon and the Salt Flats

"How I would like to believe in tenderness—"
Sylvia Plath

The moon is an ivory tusk in the Utah sky
over the salt flats of ultra white.
The ground is a soft wax that receives my steps
and prints their passage. Before the Mormons
the pulse of the earth was white, the sky, marine.
The Indians spoke of it in their red dream language
of clay and old blood. Sailing for me is the angel of
tenderness.

It had been promised in books that if I were good
and prayed to the right gods I would find my heart
netted in blue pacific light, but I'm perched
unsteadily on spindly doubts and can't run.
Winged and yet a magpie whose tail is longer than her body,
I'm clumsy when I don't talk about flying.
They call me bitter tears, Mary means,

without the trace of the sea I hear in *Maria* like a shell.
Only the salt of that forgotten ocean's biography
remains a relic of powdered bone, chalk white,
Saint Sea who still can make the earth's eyes here moist
with a keen nostalgia for it. Tears, the bed of my own making,
dry and only the salt is left behind. Watch me sleep on it.
If I could get a better look at him, I'd go to the moon

switching on her deeper lights, but the moon won't have me.
All ideas are colourless and odourless and stoppered in a vial
so that they can't be dangerous to me at this moment.
My eyes are sea green, my heart is blue.
Is it love that makes the earth pirouette on his axis
and the moon perform her crab-like bow around him?
There's no looking back, *amore,*

we're the only living things growing on the salt flats.

Don Domanski

Ironwood

a single tree
emptied of catkin and leaf
creaking in its season

a world bearing an old curse

a world of wiry twigs
in the third week of November

a kinship to the hound's jaw
aching nightly under the steps

ironwood. the crow's familiar
seated on the earth's shoulder

with no place to go
with no mouth to speak

labouring its allotment of dread
against the dispersal of cliff and sky

against the never-ending inroad
of North Atlantic weather.

Graveside

1

so this is the bleak address

where the dark elements
settle in the green fumes of the tree

where a nightwork of branches
plummets suddenly
in the wind
and the harsh rains
dissolve a geography
every other minute

so this is the bad fabric
in every tapestry
the crack in every cup

this is the hour
I always thought was here
the minutes peeling back
to reveal the unmiraculous
anxiety of this place

the little bits of death
squeezing the remaining light
to a tension
around every stone

every stick being inaccessible
every dying leaf dragging
itself away.

    2

in this light
the spirit is intolerable
full of queer personages

like this blunt tree

like these greek stars
asters
nervously bluing the air
with a clear and planetary blue
against the backdrop
of stones

the spirit is frail
at this time of day
a bowl of rose-water
full of droppings
and dead mice

overrun with bog life

there is nothing so unending as the sunrise
opening the spider's net
before the eyes

calling down the many birds
to brutalize the air.

Dreamtime

in sleep there are many radios
turned to a station
where the death taxes are paid
where the Hittites perform their slow
unpleasant songs

in sleep there are many factories
where a Gnostic might work
measuring the humility of an egg

in the place where sleep comes from
where you and I come from
there is a seaside hotel
where Sumerians dance round
a bottle of dark medicine
where Kassites sit up all night
on rocking horses made out of thumbs

in the place where sleep comes from
where you and I come from so beautifully
there is a houseboat
filled with Babylonians falling in love
with the same old story about
your thick black hair

In sleep there are many diners
where Cathars drink the coffee your mother
made for you twenty years before

in sleep there are many trains
where Canaanites read your lost mail
where Bacchantes paint the clippings
taken from your long nails
where the radio on the empty seat
sighs once to itself

sounding like a strange church
sounding like a strange season
sounding like you.

Sub Rosa

I

In each rose it is deep December. In each rose there is a
half-risen evening that never ends. There is also a dark house
full of women. Singing women on black beds. We sometimes
hear them in the waking night. We sometimes pick up their
voices while walking alone in the garden. They sound like a sea
of roses, like a harp made out of paper.

II

A rose is an unwanted place. It hangs in the garden like a spider.
It dreams of the other side. It is our enemy when we knock over
the vase, when we slam the door and move out into the night.
We begin to believe it has a face or hands making music without
desire.

III

A rose is a lion in a kingdom of lions. It is a venerable rage finally entering time. Things are not destroyed without chaos. A rose is not a rose but always a war. War in an empty house. A locked door.

IV

In profile a rose looks like a man. Full-faced it is half the sun. It avoids the quilted sound the mind makes in a thought. It avoids the proximity of the heart. It hungers after the silence between our shoulderblades or at the small of our backs. It hungers after our muteness, the dark hands in our pockets while we listen to the slap of the sea against a wall.

V

The rose speaks a dead language. Every word is a coliseum or a shoreline of broken figures. The rose is an ancient mind, the coral movement of a dead thought. It is time coming back to us. It is time churning at the end of the garden. The blue centuries full of roses and the snow falling in some future place.

VI

Let the solar rose tell its lunar tale. We will keep it secret. Let all the mystery be told like a summer's day. We will not understand. Let the hidden tide come in from the sea on a rose. The cold waters rising deep in labour.

Nocturne of Birth and Water

tonight with the sea expanding
along the vibrations of one string
with the air smelling of amnesia and salt
Death moves gracefully as a temple doll
her porcelain feet over the round
and foam-covered stones

the child says:
"Death is the first star, she rises in the east.
She has followed me over burnt ground, she has
followed me into the world. I can hear her
thoughts. Those two kettles of boiling water, those
two tumblers of bees turning over and over in
the dark."

the sea fades and folds and fades again
the fog brings the miasmic smell
of rotting kelp and half-eaten fish
with silver cataracts over all their eyes

the child floats nervously upon the water
while among the rocks the night-birds cry out
making the sound of heavy keys
along a thin brass ring.

Hammerstroke

you've driven your black sedan
just past the lines of rain
past the geranium with its red lanterns
burning late

past the stars and planets
without end

on the radio you hear the hammerstroke
that brought down the world
the awful cry that rose up once
like Caruso from his polished chair

in the backseat lives the fire
the slow nuclear night
with its tigers burning too bright
with its empty chrysalids
floating on air

outside your one headlight will last
for a thousand years
or for as long as you last
with that beam of light stiff with ghosts
that engine making random shifts
in the void

outside the nothingness will sleep
while you drive with both hands on the wheel
and the glowing dust settles in your lap

the fine blue dust that a god leaves
when it is flying toward new worlds
to be born.

Endre Farkas

Old Country Talk

You said it
or maybe me
                it doesn't matter who
one of us did declare that

There are times
              like always
when we feel as if
we are immigrants in ourselves

Why we left Where
we do not know

and even if we did
there is no choice about arriving

We are given a threadbare shape
into which we slip
as into second-hand silence

and come into this country
this perfect empty place
with used suitcases & lungs
full of foreign languages to be forgotten

The one here
is accented by fur & fire

Erotica

It is what we cannot have that is erotic;
is the silk negligee suggesting just the right amount
and it's that husky voice and slow stroke
along the curves of its absence that call you to it

It is the unknown that is erotic;
its tongue circles your nipples, closes your eyes
with its glistening slide down your chest
and begins your quest across the bridge of sighs

It is what is strange that is erotic;
its mystery is its fingers at your sex
and it has you arching in anticipation
for the new-old-sweet ache of that caress

It is the stranger who is erotic;
s/he always knows that exotic moment
when to stop and when to almost
moan "no, oh no, please/please not yet"

It is your imagination that is erotic;
stroking your lips and riding your thighs
until your senses, all so aroused
come together, come alive

The Scribe

in the morning
feeds the rabbits/ducks & chickens
keeps order among the piggish pregnant sows
saves the horse from horse-flies
has his breakfast
and goes to his studio

where he swats flies
counts swallows on the 3 wires outside his window

rolls a cigarette in secret
feels guilty

with each puff
schemes a world that is perfect
immediately gives it its independence

thinks in english of how to save the french
thinks about leaving
pauses

scratches his head & crotch
notes how the clouds are Bealy
feels subtle
             gets self conscious
edits a manuscript from b.c.

goes to the can
reads the quote on the wall
                    . . . a place of wisdom, where you clear
        the way/for drink & victuals of the coming day . . .
                                      brecht

has 3 tomato sandwiches on whole wheat
& a 50
& reads Hejda by Anaïs Nin

it is now afternoon
notates the swallows on the 3 wires   like musical score
listens to the cluck of chickens with one ear
to the music of poetry with the other

stereo

dreams of being not lonely

she   makes it quad

kills a fly
remembers Blake
is not sorry
plans ahead
counts his money
$15.00 & a mini-loto

                    money is a kind of poetry
                              wallace stevens
                              v-p Hartford Assurance

insulates his studio
knows the rain will & the cold will come in anyway
fool

inserts a new sheet into the typewriter
misspells typewriter
misspells misspells
stops

went raspberry picking
got pricked & bored
                    but thought
better these than words
kept picking/getting pricked/munched
kept an ear open for the poem
straightened my back
saw a hawk

notice the change in tense
notice the change in person

feel tired
            a poet's day is never done
            no rest for the wicked

napped

woke

intrigued by these two ordinary/everyday/unusual words
looks them up
                middle english both
stops

feeds the animals
begins to care about each sow's individuality
& notes the definite hierarchy

sups & watches french tv
       (synched *Bewitched*)
swears in french about yankeenization of canader

takes an after supper walk down a dirt road
is the fulcrum of the see-saw for the sun & moon

helps with the dishes
has 2 helpings of raspberry pie
        my/my
how things do come around

food for thought

peels an orange-orange moon
counts fire-fly lights

pisses under the stars
understand??
ends the epic

makes the night lyric

Tree Planting
with C.H.

It's about roots

matted, pulpy, delicate
lying sideways on the lawn
wrapped in temporary earth

It's about rituals

the spade & I & you
incising a holy circle

It's about digging holes

It's about right

It's about reunion

earth's black wormy love
embracing the myriad of mouths
along which the seasons' juices flow

It's about supports

It's about family

It's about stepping back
and making a silent blessing
over something that is clean

It's about washing up,
entwining

It's about flowering

[I love you]

I love you
as a way to start the poem /
always in the middle of coming
I am,
with the urgency of the everyday
with its constant changes of accent,
as figures from every walk of life who
come together on restaurant stools and
sit next to each other to share in secret rituals

I love you
in the middle of the night /
as the night shift hotel clerk who knows the beauty of chances
and who will sign in only your real name/the one we all answer to

I love you
as a close relative, by birth
by making, by death, in revolution
constantly

I love you
the song goes 24 hrs a day to simple beat
like the heart's
repeated
repeated the variations are one more than many
and are drummed across airwaves
(the beat as the messenger & message)

I love you
as a stranger to that place (love)
who, ignorant of its language,
touches only the moment's violence
and calls familiar names with new voices

I love you
as in this saint crazy labyrinth
which weaves through alleys where dreams are heaped
where sheds invite gasoline & match
where the new garden is /
next to main street
next to the mountain crowned by tombs and gray breath
but which is still sanctuary to those who embrace

I love you
as madmen their state

as madmen at the tip of the island
who stroll and stare through windows
and in each
see a naked man playing a violin

Poem Proud Papa

This is a poem of my daughter
taken with an 'olivetti Lettera 35'
months after the moon was full
and the wine so fine

You can't see her yet
(neither could we at that lyric moment)
but in the next stanza

follow closely
the journey of the moon
as it rises to full belly
through the alchemy of months
and feel her pull grow stronger
as she kicks against the form
forcing you to open,
to push and let go

Suddenly
bloody & beautiful
she is here

Raymond Filip

CANDU Can't Do

War-keeping
Not peace-keeping
Is what Canada will be noted for,
When all Halls of Fame are in flames.
CANDU's are faster than Slowpoke reactors.
CANDU's don't burp like Breeders.
CANDU's cough up twice as much weapons-grade plutonium
On a production line continuum
Than any other hot reactor
A cold war can buy.
Man-made matter,
Plutonium survives over 24,000 years.
The only other heavy element in human nature
That lasts longer is love.

One kilogram of plutonium
Spilled across the planet,
As rope-a-dope radioisotopes,
Could fillet the lights
Out of every man, woman, and androgyne,
In twenty minutes, twenty months, twenty years,
Depending upon metabolism.
Cremate a contaminated body,
Radiation just shimmies up the chimney
To snuff more standing stock of humanity.
How can you trust an ethical code
Which calls lethal waste "bonus material"?
Or an accident "normal aberration"?
Normal aberrations that give birth to
Human fruit flies,
Leak leukemia into babyblood,
Strontium 90 into bones,
Cause freaky mutations in animals:

Frogs with three legs,
Rats with two heads,
Lemmings with no eyes.
The Peaceful Atom never delivered
"Energy too cheap to meter."
The Peaceful Atom murders uranium miners
With radioactive radon gas mine tailings.
The Peaceful Atom provides plutonium
For international games of Chicken.
At the bottom of the Peaceful Atom
Spy Mackenzie King bowing
To wartime ally Tube Alloy secrets:
Montreal wing of the Manhattan Project.
Minutemen won't be swift enough.
NATO, NORAD, ICBM, FOBS, SAC, RDF,
Need Microsecondmen!
There is no dearth of death on earth.
Our biosphere belches one big chemical casino:
Killer compounds of carbon monoxide,
Carbon dioxide, sulphur dioxide, nitrogen oxide;
Hydrocarbons, microwaves, macrodust;
Cosmic fraternities of Alpha, Beta, Gamma
Radiation roving in ultraviolet violence.
The world will inhale on odd days,
Exhale on even days.
Somebody should invent a bomb
That only bumps off politicians.

As long as money remains the prime mover:
Skinned, gouged, bled, laundered,
Nuclear reactors make expensive wart removers.
AECL, AECB, ENL, UCL, plus Hydro utilities
Are not immune to expansion for pedigreed greed
In place of practical need.

If medicine can be socialized,
So can energy.
Cost of alternative sources
Would skydive astronomically.
Or else beam your future
Solar heating bills
To Imperial Esso Sunlight.
Whosoever says selling nuclear technology
To backward foreign governments
Balances trade deficits
Must promise to dance in the fallout.
Bilateral agreements are pieces of paper.
The Kremlin sifted through SALT II
To pepper Afghanistan.
"Reaganomics" means Reaganatomics.
All the *prana* power
Plus ashram enlightenment
In India did not deter
Trombay Nuclear Research Station
From premeditated detonation
Of Hinduism's first A-bomb,
With Canadian uranium.

If a peaceful life is too much to ask for,
Let us not fear more than a peaceful death.
Plutonium is not a mere bronchial buster.
Plutonium is the show stopper.
Plutonium, Pluto, God of Death.
Finally,
Something new under the sun:
Another sun,
Where the earth was.

The Mighty Buck, the Immigrant Fuck, and Melting Pot Luck

Right off the boat, or Boeing,
I admit being tongue-tied.
For I am the language that is lost,
The name that is changed,
The ghost of welcome houses and Saturday schools.
I am men in sheepskin coats from the Old Country;
I am their New Country descendants: women in Persian lamb.
I am Euro-paeans:
Songs you won't sing and dances you won't dance.
I am hard money.
I am the inalienable right to alienation.
The Horatio Alger Algerian, the Haitian electrician,
The Cuban security guard, the cab driver from Calabria,
The Jewish landlord who lives in Florida,
The Vietnamese orphan, the Romany musician.
I am Hutterite, Mennonite, Wahabite, Bahai, Sikh, and Alcoholic.
I am the Canadian Mosaic: a melting pot on ice.
I am always the next generation,
The child with which good immigrant fiction ends.
I am that child grown up, writing in English,
Mother tongue in mind, adopted tongue in cheek.
You were Commonwealth, I am common loss.
Like a citizen of the world, in exile,
Or an overseas package returned to sender,
I am nothing left to be but Canadian.

Never Marry an Artist

Never marry an artist,
Unless you like starving,
Or eating after immortality.
They're softer than peanut butter melting in the sun,
And just as rich, and smooth, and nutty.

Never marry an artist.
Uncivil and disobedient,
Civil servants can't make heads or tails of them.
They're a curiosity, a brown bag.

Never marry an artist.
There's no money in it.
They're losers.
Marry a critic, or a culture vulture:
The winners, the failed artists.

Never marry an artist.
They're ineligible bachelors,
In knots before you even tie one.
You won't be a golf widow,
You'll be a frisbee widow.
Life will part you worse than death.

Never marry an artist.
They'll divorce themselves from reality
On the grounds of mental cruelty.
They'll carry you over the threshold
Of a new consciousness.

Never marry an artist.
Niagara Falls will roar against it.
They'll want every street they have laughed
And danced and sang on to bear their name,
But be lucky to wind up a number
In some nameless asylum.

Never marry an artist.
Unless you can grow as their gift of communication
Grows in community with you.

Marry an artist,
If you can say:
I don't.

My Sister, My Self

We learned to tie our own shoelaces,
Then walked out on each other.
Neither of us wears
Our father's name.
No family crystal
To gather for our gaze,
Our heritage is a history of walls:
As cold as The Iron Curtain,
As broken as The Brandenburg Gates,
As closed as Quebec Language Barriers.
No models but a muscular mother
Tough as prayer book leather.

Two tiny tots nine hot dogs high,
How we hugged each other with nightmares,
Not even inner space to protect us
From dormant monsters with daddy's face.
Fittingly reunited, future shock years later,
By the loss of that father, feather, führer.
A family more fractured than the fault lines
Of the collision between *Europa* and North America.
My sister and I can't look at Old Country pictures
Of roses and rosaries reposed on dead relatives,
Dropped into our lives
Like leaves from sacred oaks.

Out of left-over love,
We re-discover what it is
To be sister and brother,
Trade a dahlia for a kiss,
Hesitant to touch hands.
Her warmth is
The sum of summer.
Her eyes,
Blue of my blue,
A doll found in the river.

Roof Garden

Even if the flowers could not fill a girl's skirt,
Even if the roof bears more garbage than a beergarden,
Even if the earth was bought at Woolworth,

It is still my garden, my asylum.
The neighbor's children avoid midget marigolds
Without being told, sensing a private beauty
In the charmed rectangle of petals which must not be harmed.
My green-eyed cat falls asleep faster in this kitty corner,
Her miniature forest, secure from beasts of the street.
Down below,
Some animal driving a Trans-Am
Had busted her hind leg plus my budget.
Having worked out her balance of terror,
The fussy sleeper now naps on her back,
Bad leg up in the air.
And my rogue geranium
Has also risen
In these rougher pastures.
Revived with Perrier
After a zero growth winter,
The white leaves were papery as price tags.
I placed the lifeless plant
Upon the highest spot on the house,
A floral finial.
Buds burst like botanic bombs
Blushing crimson and carmine.
That tough old geranium taught me
Gentleness is the hardest thing.

Above urban blight,
I tap my typewriter for words
Tender and strong as wings
Which hold up the sky.
I sweep away blossoms and dust,
Small claims to my care,
Which lend the sunset its colors.

Softening to Heaven

Aušros Vartai (Our Lady Gate of Dawn) is a legendary shrine located in Vilnius, the capital city of Lithuania. Theurgical lore concerning the curing powers of its icon arose with the aerial roots of religion. Between 1671-1761 seventeen major miracles were documented beyond reasonable doubt. This medieval marvel of survival has also evolved into a political symbol of salvation.

A dievdirbys is a "god maker," carver of wayside crosses or sacred sculptures. No longer visible, over eight thousand of such works of faith have been torn down by USSR ministries.

Hard to believe
A bas-relief of Our Lady Gate of Dawn:
Dark countenance with darker hands that crisscross
A pure aurora of gold folds like sandbars at Palanga.
Silver hearts incrust her starry cope
For every cure over three centuries of mirabilia.
The Savior was born in a manger,
Not a bank vault.
Very easy
To make fun of fundamentalism,
Holy Russophobia.
Harder to mystify the iffy,
Or to magnify the masses as Messiah.

On a goose step of private ground,
Where prayer is an act of rebellion,
My grandfather, "the god maker,"
A *dievdirbys*, built a cross with class.
That crucifix saw the flux
Of my mother running with the ravens
From the *Russkis* in 1940;
Saw Nazis chop churches into chuckholes;
Saw freedom fighters massacred by the acre in Red forests;
Saw the Soviet hammer descend on granddad's dream farm
Like a doghouse because his pride had refused to live
In a plow to plow and cow to cow collective.
By safe conduct of some spare spirit,
One tree, rooting that one rueful rood,
Survived reconstruction into communist firewood.
Fifty years later in an empty field,
I leaped up to touch the tiny majesty of his totem,
Exalted that a higher goal than production ceiling
On potatoes had inspired grandpapa
To put up that last cross.
A morning's work of carpentry,
A miracle enough for me.

Vilnius/Sakiai
Lithuania
1983

Dan Jalowica

Judith Fitzgerald

holy water
for v.c.

i love your consecration
your sacramental slant
the way you blessed my skin
i couldn't miss
the delicious surrender to pleasure
the thirteen stations so oblique
and understated;
my love's under-rated
for you, being unique,
a kind of ship-wrecked treasure
in an under-water kiss
where the smoulder should begin
our nerve ends resonant
in champion blue hesitation

i love your consecration
in champion blue hesitation
your sacramental slant
our nerve ends resonant
the way you blessed my skin
where the smoulder should begin
i couldn't miss
in an under-water kiss
the delicious surrender to pleasure
a kind of ship-wrecked treasure
the thirteen stations so oblique
for you, being unique,
and understated;
my love's under-rated

step father

he sheltered nothing /
intent on her learning
silence, priming the slow
progress into the dark woods,/
he forced her to watch
while he delicately placed
shells in small animals
and left chewed red cartridges
buried in spruce needles
on the dark green floor

she learned that
she couldn't escape
his vicious attack
on animals and trees /
and stopped hearing
his voice, he silenced her
at ten in the bush;/
placed the axe's edge
with skilled precision
in the forehead of her dog

her silence never broke,
each time his monstrous hands
would clamp axe and carve
into dark spruce she watched
the way they always fell;
he cut into her childhood
his huge hand /
over her mouth/
her small body impressed
in needles on the dark green floor

Energy

begins where
it leaves off, constantly
coming full circle
to forget itself
before

there is no escape
except in the refuge
of this poem, hide
here, discover the awful
lie, you can take it
with you
when you finally rest

even when you're over
as self, your self
rises up and asserts you;
covers every ground
for the hazard
of your existence, gives
shape to the after-
self, allows dispersion
to gather each molecule
in its vast uniting storm

touch of zygosis

my husband's camera is a thing
I rarely understand, though it teaches me
daily I am learning about our union—
our plateau—out of place but in focus
so close to placebo sometimes that even I
must catch my breath and snap the necks
of fragile hours
and location, situation convulsive, spasms
back faster than the need of night

I wanted to set our surroundings
down gently, though I am not your average
photographer, knowing little about fast and slow,
about light,
about metre, for the life of me
I've never forgiven those tiny numbers
on the lens, the sophisticated mechanisms
that transform outer space
to a one-dimensional trick of place

this small act of modern magic, I believed
was what a conjugation needed, some verified
relic, an invasion by privacy
of all things; I wanted the natural relation
of our lives to our situation, to capture
the essence of place, even though it is
continually rearranging itself without much
interference from gametangiums

I began with a small area, the chair
with the quilted cushion, the open shutters
splashing the square pieces of light
on the gypsymoth fluttering in the book
left open; I understand
that purpose and precision are not always
as simple as they sound

however, they work in photographs

with one eye on the moment and the other
against Sisyphus, knowing I
wasn't going to get caught in a futile boulder
syndrome, not me
I am at least as competent a photographer
as Narcissus, with as much suspended disbelief
as the next girl, I clicked the camera's whip
and for a moment thin as wings
I was inside the camera and the gypsymoth
was photographing herself

so much film and conjugation
depending on the angle

mouth to mouth recitation

who, indeed? the question rips my mouth
and tears off a bouquet of blood-cosmic roses;
petals fluttering and exploding in
the passionate calm of angels, since those
angels are taller than tales, than takes
and mistakes, than angel breaks

mild fabulous angels
in the pounding shock
of rilke's disenchantress
resounding and rounding the edge
of terrestrial knowing:
only a glance
roses growing

the violin from the unnerving open window
crescendos through pure lyrical refrains;
roses open their incredible eyes
and animate fabulous angel strains,
the bow cuts through thick air: a knife

blossoming serrated symphonies
from an indifferent world-heart
not to interpret roses
but to accelerate
breathless art

effectively coming through slaughter

for Michael Ondaatje

as I see it

what began as vague premonition
became something passionate, became
possession and never considered
release; there's no catharsis in this
procession, this parade down
the clear cutting street

    there's pain, prostitution
pushing limits to their limits, scar
slashed pickett, pimp par excellence

there's unlimited belief in sight
seeing is believing
there's no relief in night
stars, in blues bars, in the arsenal
of buddy's scars

            self-
            inflicted
            or
            straight-
            razored

there's magnets, their properties
also premonition, their own spinning
of the web, the spiders ranging
out into the hot street, shot with
threats, oceans of blood, cities of sweat
boxes of ice, there's a sweet secrecy
of knowing
of showing
off-beat
there's a threat and there's an answer
there's a throat and there's an answer
speechless

        walking into the answer

retreating in the photograph, receding
until sheer notes rip across windowing

              fire

shattering into perfect flame

and it was windows
       windows
       windows
       windows
       windows
       windows

and sometimes

      suicided stars

gaping from the sockets of a siren
gathering in a wail of perfect clarity

20/20 vision
seeing the air
as an entity, an offering

sometimes even the enemy
opposite breath

it comes all the way back to here
in this conception, this magnet
the clue, the formal madness, buddy's
yoking of self to other
               to animal
                slaughter

freeze: frame
flesh: flame

formless as ice
tense as order
still

will consume as a mirror

because I was flesh
I was my worst fear

Sunday Morning

It's Sunday morning and foggy;
what are you doing
for the rest of your life? Are you
interested in becoming
a participant in the passion
my mourning embraces?

Are you looking
for me? Open your hands,
your eyes, our accidents
are occurring in them
with the frequency of stars
in the *holy hush* of illicit, imperfect time.

I dream a little; the fog yields
to intervals of heart beat
and reminiscence; to the procession
of the living, distilled in the longing
that binds my molecules and atoms
into the shape of loving I have become.

Are you restless and similarly dreaming
of traffic and passion and visions and wheels?
Do you know the extent of this calm darkness
that rubs against me,
that severs the static electricity
from the divinity within you?

"All pleasures and all pains, remembering"
your presence, instilled in three
miraculous days and nights and dazes
that burst into consciousness; that cover
my need for you in the absolute fog condition:
that it blunt the edge of seeing.

Doug Weller

Artie Gold

[Sun filters through my window]

Sun filters through my window
velvet like bats' bellies the shadows it casts
flutter about my room. I share the unrest

the sun is doomed with; the movement
sunup sundown moving around: ground sky ground
its only comfort the habit of its orbit.

we are orbs whatever we do is behaviour
the truth of our moment is too predictable
yet I delight in the sun.   it is monumental

in the sky with certainty rising, setting
looking to the greater cycle, there is colour,
a yellow angel pedals about the world.

[The poem I am writing]
for Ken Jimenez

The poem I am writing
is Charles Ives, standing thinking
his second Piano Sonata

    this is moving from him in its performance

there is little else of this piece
  he has left others to fuddle with;
just the gentle old man
thinking and humming
beside a piano river.

The piano is the poem itself, not
an instrument of background
if there were to be a landscape
with the river a single line on it,
maybe a rag doll , with the patches
blown up to be separate fields
and farms .
he plays it in Bucks County,
for it seems to me and him
that America
    happened most there .

sex at thirty-one

Is like love at seventeen. it plies deep
Affords the illusion there is nothing else.

Every few years kicks sand in the face of everyfew years
Love, only a pornography of the heart has a habit of being

Waylaid, it had a habit of suddenly throwing down
Its basket of roses and running. rape, basic call of thing

Changed. suddenly and love dies like drool on a napkinless chin
Love gives way to one of love's perversions. dry skin

To wetness. even the idea of sex glistens. like the heart
Thinking of where it left its bubblegum. the heart

Is a dry old taskmaster. its puppies are like the grains
of sand dragged on to a picnic blanket. as the afternoon

Turns into death. count love with a slight chill. too many
Times love has occurred, reared its beautiful head. we are sick

Sick of change. sick of wind change. sick of lifeguard change
Sick of the tides of the heart.

alison

I am alerting you to the fact that the clouds
above your house are doing a dance THIS MINUTE
   and if I wait, well. . .

but I have already waited, a human faculty, thinking
   what if the clouds by the time you have woken
have flown, disarranged themselves. gone to Europe

I juggled this thought unconscious of the lapse of time
while the clouds stayed and stayed. now the clouds can't say:
   c'mon, Artie, wake her up. we are here only briefly

or Artie the day is glorious, take your time, ponder
   this human condition you talk of. we are here
at your beck. we are like the photo of beautiful day

drawn from the textbook of surrealism, surrealism,
the everyday that never happens. and the clouds are gone.
a personal experience. which for you, never was.

so I leave a note on your doorstep; alison, wake up—
the clouds can be beautiful!

[I have been thinking]

I have been thinking a great deal
about my bike that will be stolen.

I don't like things whose inevitability
works against me.

Why have you driven through my heart?
Make that   what.

Old Road Song Poem

I have no astrologer—
and don't believe in falling in love
on any particular August day you could name

I have knapsacks full of knick-knacks
that spread beneath a tree
would suffocate a hermit

and a perpetual cough
that when I've had enough of—
I'll die from.

I came to this city
naked   and from a small town
and have rearranged some of its objects

I will hitch-hike out of here one day
with my hair in my eyes and a good breeze blowing
and cause a little confusion I'm sure—

though no more than a hair
discovered in a gravy.

[I don't have the energy for another day]

I don't have the energy for another day
like a poor hand of scrabble without vowels. . .
the sun is at my throat

I wonder what sense I am making of human history
getting halfway through the day leaving a poem scrawk

just thinking about why I fail
screws me right in there
we have a sense of tradition

like watery spaghetti. .

it is the poorer countries that I wonder about; there,
energy abounds. It is their gift to get ahead
to feel lousy doing it; mine
    to slip   and
to have one hell of a banquet:

  roast corpse of the western world. something must fill a hole—
or what is the dirt dying for?

I call this rarefied morality
some days I can shoot it in my veins without my conscience flinching
these days I slide off without batting an eyelash.

Relativity of Spring

I.

The nouns are hungry for sense
The facts are not known
They are tasteless by which is meant
They are hard to trancribe
They taste the colour of the sky against cement
They appeal silently as apples might
and their bodies crawl like turtles with shells
and they fall taking sun to the ground on them.

Yipping like dogs they crawl being blistered in the sun
on the back of the dolphin a caress touches like an alarm
cancer of the colon, the skin
tendril of the bone's sensuality.

The dark dirty dishwater of an x-ray plate
The queen's love throws the first pitch
It reveals the hidden
It sings into activity
telling garbage from submerged fish
and dreams

Water's sudden edge
bell's flower
for the sun to be useful to its breathing
for the sight who loses sequence in art
he comes up with what chemicals it will provide
she watches her replacement
we the complex lobster wearing animal pelt
we the gods describe this earth totally
where the sharks can never really come is totally our own
where this takes place is our authority.

The air's barely acceptable sending of sound
The queen's idea throbs like starmatter
no one wasting words outside of speech
no one worries hard stone
the surprise in one's voice not heard from passing back to oneself.
The boards of the palace are grained.

II.

I dance like air in autumn
I house like shadow
mercenary of breath
shortcircuiter of meadow
Each season I arrange orthogonally
Each semicircular jar I denote pleasurable
In the marketplace of chrome dwarfs
In the ring of deserts
In the feelings of scorned women reaching out to trap this society
The whips of each jealousy reaching chords deeper than music
These days are hard to endure going through submarine time
These policemen strike into fear itself

I am the cauldron of bowling prowess
I am the crying one who is struck
I am like a greatness whose ass even pirates must kiss
and I am exactly worrying, hesitation
The double versatility of early intent
The pompous exaltant baboon
was like a mastery aced
was like a spectacle too ugly to behold
before dying it shook my hand like three tired popes
before dying it strutted pretending to thank me
The passport is subject to unholy fits

The mountain is climbed sorrowfully
Get here this moment on your knees
Go out slowly but towards joy
crawling along the broken glass of your mistakes
a cautious second life.
No one has to love life even
just to continue living.

III.

Now come through a beating of pasts
born so as to miss my vote.
It is when through a slant that it begins with bitter purity
and by some chance bitching gets it a poetry
into pallid flung arms they boldly set to
coming full circle in some mind's interchange
and each comes into an encampment of its own.
With its arrival the year is splintered into ten thousand months
To kill something aleatory from my bitter cache
thinking perhaps by this action to arrive at one spring.

It is certain the typed characters dog in shame
fuses follow them like tails, hissing in guilt
before which cult I bear greetings of change
the necessary amount of steps must be walked
we are as wanted as any drug
as dangerous as two colds from one source.

R. W.

Beauty will drink a toast at my wanton destruction (an event)/
disclosing the cumbersomeness of my race like a rotting commode
a tractor tries to outdistance / but is chained to by blood.

Had we this. had we that. . imploringly we feed.   I should have
                                                                    loved
your double standard. . if need could invent love;   here we have
/ bad blood / here we dream.   Sending monsters into our Tokyo.
The sun sets against the idea of caves thinking to have found a
                                                                    ledge.
In the mornings. . Mozart and Villon, the singular of caress, *cares*. .

We think we have stumbled on the sudden and secular secret that
                                                                    will
  just for us   unlock worlds,   well, won't it? the morning runs off
and like an oxbow lake small life is stranded in these stagnant
                                                                    pools
the blood in our minds, goes stale while the salt of life without/
  even becoming precious, concentrates to burn us where we've
                                            chosen to make our stands.

Joanne Jackson Johnson

Kristjana Gunnars

changeling VIII

every morning i break trail
down the mountainside
big snowflakes muffle my bootsteps
like cold skin
on invisible faces
trying to talk

i, too, suffocate under my name
i can't live
up to my great grandmother's ghost
i want another easier name

name me weevil
so i can prowl at night
name me grey mountain carpet moth
so i can hide
name me harvestman
i want to scavenge before daylight

i don't want to have to apologize
for the red mites on my legs
name me harvestman because my mother
dreamed bugs when i lay in her
heath, bracken, birch bugs
she dreamed worms, grey & red
with flat tails & ripples of spine

she dreamed i burrowed through the damp wall
the humus floor
broken & suffocating even then
at the threat of being

born under great grandmother's majesty
under the white headdress

don't give me a hard life
don't make me die young
give me another name
more suitable

name me leech
name me woodlouse
name me a dream i dream
name me broadleaved woods

monkshood XXI

it doesn't take long
it's always sudden & afterwards
you sit in a purple hood
in the cellar & wait

in a white-plastered hall
single-minded, unadorned

youth is monkshood

girls read friar's cap texts
on wolfsbane benches
along the wall
echoes rustle with turning pages

a sunray streaks into a corner
gray-shaded
all beginnings have an end
end has an end too

an opening
pale green leaves
shady sites by water
country escapes
hooded robins on unbranching stems

youth is a clean blue silence
no voice, no wing
youth is an hour of reading

it doesn't take you long
soon again you get to go
footsteps sound on hollow floorboards
if it's an accident—
no need to be morose

they let you out to finish the plan
your lifespan
youth is part of an afternoon
numb with monkshood
aconite waiting

but then you step out
in the end

monkshood XXIII

in tollund fen they fed you barley
linseed, knotweed, sixty-three grains
hanged you, drowned you
in peat humus in midwinter
to bring on spring

so they did to tollund man
& he rose again in 1950
with worms' eggs in his guts
whiskers on his chin
rope around his neck

spring is over now
three of us bike in high summer
gitte, jytte & i
stop at the farms for water in the heat

& at tollund fen we tilt our bikes
against an aging dogwood
at a rush-covered hut
immersed in alders

a yellow-faced farmer hands us a jug
to dip into the well
& the courtyard soil is waterlogged
after the morning rainflash

we drink under the thick alder
turn by turn & i notice
the farmer braced against his doorpost
whiskered & bent over
searching out our time from his heathen place

monkshood XXIX

my great grandmother & her mother
& her mother before her
waited here in the ancient ruin
of danehof castle, waited

to emerge from blindness
out of a dark time

this is my icon
my window into truth

the tower is empty
the bench where they stared in brown silence
lines the wall, deserted
& i fill the vacancy for a moment
sit in their seat
in a dank room

looking out i can tell my pupils
are enlarged because of darkness
not nightshade
not black cherry juice
that women distilled in the middle ages

a roman cosmetic
to dilate the eyes
to make them belladonnas

the red-veined coronas are the stained glass
& outside the women's blindness
lies ruined in the nightshade

wakepick I

tonight i disentangle
soft underwool fibre from coarse hairs
make ready for carding

rain blasts at the membrane window
the mud walls are damp
begin to leak, little by little
onto the sleeping benches

i escape this flood in the work of hands
pretend not to see the paste
of whiteflies trod underfoot
into the soft mud floor
pretend not to feel clammy & cold

we have no use for human fleas
no use for bland horsehair & wool

tonight again i pretend
to be salt
i separate myself again
fine from coarse
die another death tonight

& when i'm dead
i turn to knotweed on the knolls
to starlings in the rain
i turn blood, hair, bone
i turn to stone

in the work of my hands
i turn my fragments up from the floor
blood & bone from the floor
make ready for another rain
tonight again

i disentangle sinew, hair
i turn to stone

the dots of de dondi

I do not think we have listened enough to the clocks
we do not often remember
the heartbeat of time began in 1362
with Giovanni de Dondi's
mechanical *masterpiece*

replica of the human mind
how it told time
& showed the movement of the planets
de Dondi de Dondi de Dondi, nor do we
stop to consider

such brains were manufactured four
centuries later, refined
elegant celestial globes
of domestic utility

Our time here is a matter of lines
carefully arranged in a space of no lines
I do not think we have viewed them closely enough
they are made of dots

never before have we whispered among ourselves
how our lifespan has become
an American crayon drawing

coalface universe

you know it is time to begin
again, the universe is
enormous, imaginary space
dealt out in zeros, casual
numbers, thousands, millions

but you begin, crayon & ink
wash, draw a new pattern on
an old canvas, there
inside your skull you prepare
studies, sculptures where
the world is, we know

there are wars, people hide
in subway shelters, in
mines, there is the cramped
view into space along narrow
lives. a motley text-
ure of an old civilization

where you know you must begin
over. the brain is
curdled, broken dots group
where dreams once spread
out, your own expanding galaxies
wash down now

Brian Henderson

February Margins

(St. Valentine's Day, 1980)

Almost no
snow this year
birds in a feast of seeds
Recognition comes only
with loss

Redpolls would have opened
small dark spaces for our breathing
in the field of white

We are left, however, with
ice, the blizzard of light
its naked toil, noose
as if for a rabbit on this small trail

Your arms fold impossible
blankets of light
The glare of ground is eaten away
beneath my feet

It is hard, cold, invariable
that swallows birds without comment
and whole trees in its pour

Fears breed in our bed, like crystals, nations
are crushed with terrible refraction
Its beauty is appalling, a
holy war, *jehad*, that pulls the darkness out
of the brain's bulb
like the amaryllis

We would read the limits of ourselves
in the extravagant migration of light

3rd Migration, Third Series

I

What listens? The deluge of light
is roaming, preoccupied, under the earth
Sky is an impenetrable foliage
hung with deaf fruit. Only the dead hear

but they are such absolute listeners
drawing everything out of me, reaching down
through my throat into the soft gardens of organs,
are so real, I need to be, must be among them

A demon from the Book of the Dead, suicide
in a chair, fabriced with Persian birds
I'm anchored at the end of the night

But it's you I remember, your breath
forgetting to cloud the air, perfectly,
who went through with it early, and was right all along

(for J.D.)

II

To write is a suicide. Not
to write, once having started
is also a suicide
How private is this public garden

the speechless hummingbird addressing
the blood reds of the hollyhocks
leaves turning their bountiful and green ears
their odd mouths, audience of clouds

This writing: earth, the body
of earth, her darkness, her swaths
of light, blooming, and demanding

dead. Or Berryman addressing
his God: *riotous doubt assailed me*
Wee have prayed unto you and ye have not. . .

III

"Sorrowful yet serene waves," over the radio
Sky. No. No. I'm listening, yes
Yes. That change. The unrecognizable's terrifying
But no one but the mad and the dead can change
so purely. But
                    not to change is to remain
only half human.
                    Afraid, perhaps of finding myself
empty. Know the hollow tree, *husk of
hands*. Waves of panic, facing the weather
of words, laughter, and worst of all, the sheer

precipice of silence, that loss
of connection, sudden beginning of awareness and
awkwardness
knowing I should say something. . .

But the stoney river bed the sky sleeps in
listen, is speaking for me

IV

Continue with the impossible, living
together, though we speak different languages
Our heritage of difference. The sun
keeps pulling itself out of the landscape

doesn't it? Even this far north.
And this morning, the magnolia warbler
the cat got, breast still
bright yellow in my hand. Shed light:

Déblocage. So that change might begin within. . .
that reign of longing for whatever home might be
I put our letters down, impossibly

The body's just violence or tenderness
But the political debacle that love is:
You have to name the changes to get them happening

V

That bird you dreamt of, nightmare from another time
its float, annulled flight, emptying, like
the condor, intangible shadow across your thought
was only me, with flung-out arms, wanting

to hold you. Lift of your blue lake, of your
mountains, there could be no flight without
The higher the flying, the more the needed earth
is felt. Or that was my half of the dream

Vigil, matching them now, bound to caring
the difficult human shift. Moving. Enduring
Images. Candor of each other's dreams

The opening seams, rends, appears, and holds
finally together the metamorphosis of love
and this: Inca praise in the updrafts, your coastlines

VI

Day of the Mothers. Storms all night, wanting
to collapse the sky
                          bury us in a drift of stars
My dreams wandering like lightning, fall-out
from a life lived with fear, the margin of words

all the inexorable separations that triumph. Being
at a loss
            to leave or to stay, to speak or to remain
silent. Wind
                pushes at the windows
                                            Sun
spreads through the room
                            now while you dress, like a voice

I section the orange for our breakfast
                                        We've come all this way
for the migrating birds, are
                            ourselves migrants
the secret female places begin, conceive of

that risk: holding and losing at once
                                    Today
tongues are buds
                    the poplar leafing its hearts
the hackberry with its bright, temporary fruit of warblers

VII

Today: utter earth, utter sky
only this always appearing

The hummingbird's seam
of flight over the current hedges
cataract of honeysuckle. . .

As kids we caught them at the mouths of hollyhocks
until their red throats seemed to burn through our hands

And to the Aztecs, these nectar
drinkers were the souls of the dead
who sacrifice themselves, willingly

How the gods, Tezcatlipoca, needed
us, to nourish this hungry, unstable
and always vulnerable home

that a word you don't sound could send awry

A White Wall under the Wallpaper

Winter berries, orange, red; seedpods, and
wooden flowers against the drift of
meaning, its sudden white-out. The cold breaks
your breath when it leaves you. You wonder how
it keeps coming. The mind dozes in its
cradle of snow, perfect obedience
The smudge of sun, a smear of light on grey
is a memory of a thing you can't
quite grasp. Under the white paint, the rich rose
hues of gumwood perhaps. What you meant by
not getting the words right. The snow reveals
its blizzard of freedom right to the
horizon. It obliterates all tracks
leaving, clearly, nothing to go on

Walking through the Door

The metaphor, if really lived, derealizes
the world, and only the metaphor
is real. The metaphor holds the earth
back, holds it, and itself, fares forward
with an almost absolute sense
of wonder
          and also nostalgia
as of the still living lives of
the dead in us, those
we have left behind forever

Forever
who gather
us

the way the sun, going under, gathers
all colour to itself
and gives it to the sky

Vertigo

Perhaps it was a thousand years ago, but you knew me once. Now the words condense like a sweat, a humid necklace on me. Flesh slurs to wax. I'm not mentioning the falcon dream, or the star your body became. Soft reckless light in the room falls away, a body punished and diminishing. If there are always two, I double up with pain, or laughter. The black table-cloth is a dense star absorbing the stain of our memories. I can't recall something about us. The emptiness sees itself in everything, but that must be why we're here. No one is speaking. The tree by the table gives you a leaf for a mouth. We are in the Mexico of the imagination, a lost childhood by the tree of skulls, and sniffing the wet smoke of burning hearts. A land from which someone, radiant, comes back with skull-fruit, as the bone has its flower of flesh. We don't even *have* to speak. Your floor, I notice, is a roof of clouds.

Investiture

This song is dangerous. It prays and draws blood. It grabs things by the hair and flings them one by one and one after another onto the dark stone. *Chac-mool* looks blankly out at the splendid city and the floating gardens from the left, over there by the Hummingbird. What does it all float on? *Tlaloc* mists the parched valleys and somewhere places dew on the cactus, while priests sing their monotonous songs, their matted hair dipped in blood. The earth invests in blood. It is a flame as sharp as obsidian knives. One arm to the black north, one to the blue and unpredictable south; feet to the crimson dawn, and head to the house of women in the white west. I open ribs like a book, tear out the heart in one motion and lift it in my hand, flopping like a landed fish, up to the sky. Nothing changes; rather things continue, or better, always begin again. If only things weren't so tenuous, needed us so badly to stay, to hover as if real, or to take on the shining instant of motion they are over and over again when we nourish them. And we are always called to this: the ownership of our nature: the informing and deforming truth we are the children of. Her name is *Coatlique* and she is dangerous. You see we are already dead; only the god lives in us. We have to make a space for that. And it is wonderful and terrible too if the universe is to breathe. And I am afraid because always I must hazard what I love most deeply, and in dreams I see the gods themselves rolled crashing down the great steps of the temple in the darkness.

Diane Keating

Summer Solstice

To lie motionless, a lizard
the sun piercing my skin
light rushing through the green
wilderness, my body.

To run across meadows, mud
under my feet for cures
my thighs ensuring
crops and fat cattle.

To dig forgotten messages
from the roots of white oak
my shade folding into a crow
crying *too far, too far.*

To soar through my mind
leaving broken mirrors—
shadowless, free, I'm lost
in these splinters.

Mad Apples

Baba Yaga, Baba Yaga
by my belfry of ribs
my altar of hair
help me, My Lady of Lilies
lock me in stained glass
a chapel without doors.

>   Daughter you must go to the suburbs
>   wash on Mondays, arrange on Fridays.

Baba Yaga, Baba Yaga
by sweating shadow
bleeding cloud
help me, O Maid of Mad Apples
make the Prince blind
as the moon at midday.

>   Daughter you must go to the malls
>   consume the days. . .

Baba Yaga, Baba Yaga
by hood of hawks
skin of angels
help me, O Witch of the Wingless
to live behind glass
where gold light meets black air.

>   My daughter you must go to the Prince.
>   The tower is a bungalow on asphalt acres.
>   The tower, your heart.

Mooncalf I

I saw a woman
sew the sky
into a dress.
I saw the sun
drop in a beggar's cup
a rainbow
garrotte a swan

but the only man
I met
threw knives—
moonlight
through my eyes.

Leda Forgets the Wings of the Swan

Your images shift around me.
Humpbacked and white
they resemble death.

Your eyes raise towers higher.
At the edge of the pond
your neck's a question mark.

My mouth opens to your fiery tongue
that I may be mute to the light,

my thighs for your pleasure
that angels may worship.

Dream Master, that I may find
who I am, let your flushed beak
tear at my heart and mind.

II

Blood must come before love.

*To break the mirror
I break myself.*

*Astonished
I body out into wholeness,
reaching into the blue oracular air.*

O halfmoon man, my scars ache.

Fecundity

I'm a walled orchard.
Fruit swells
inflamed by the evening.

I ache for your bite,
to have water, fire,
sucked from me.
Outside the gates
I hear swans rutting.

I want to be pinned
to the hot earth,
my cry splitting
the moon, juice and seed.

God, how I long for stars
to mark where
I've taken you in.

Boxcars

A trackless moon
moving the night.
Our palms converge.
The lines pull souls
from their sockets.

We stare out the window
at the first star
stationed between chimneys.

Desire pulls us down lines
like a boxcar
that binds this nickel town
to the Big Dipper. Later you say
More than blood
moves through the heart.

We wait at the station.
Boxes of fallen stars
shunt along the track
that shines before us.

Flower Song

Aw come on
desire's no defeat.
I'm your orchid
with the tunnel to heaven.

Come on boy
don't force me into a bottle
like a pink-toed bat.

Let my tongue be the wick
and we'll take
the shape of fire.

Among the ash
you'll find my heart,
a peach stone.

Summons for the Undead

Gray clouds in the east, bare wings
to carry the moon's severed head.

> *Wolf behind the barn, howl*
> *Wind through the keyhole, groan*
> *Awaken the life imprisoned in stone.*

Pink clouds in the west, mushrooms
to poison the sun's fierce heart

> *Snake under the stairs, hiss*
> *Robins on the roof, sing*
> *Awaken the dead imprisoned in skin.*

Glory Be To God
For Dappled Things

Putty fills the horizon
smoothing sky into earth.

I sway in a hammock
under golden apples
watching monarch butterflies
bicker like bewitched children
among frilly edges of shade.

In the thick stillness
clouds gather.
My body becomes a cocoon,
my heart, writhing wings.

I await your dark claw.

Erin Mouré

Fantastic World's End

What else can you do, faced
with yourself   day in & out
The bottles near you, a sense
of accomplishment burned in your dream:
Out of bottles you pour   the sad
huzzahs of strangers, filling stomachs & tongues

What else can you do:
the damaged brain knocks on the room's face,
the room falls down,
the Christ crawls back into his mother's soft womb,
bleating like a lamb

It's said there are
those who don't know the self's refusal,
the gravity that nails the tongue shut like a shoe,
the force, whatever it is,
that halts the hand's caress
& makes us civil, empty-headed, sentient   beings

What hate is,
what fear is,
to feel the same ache pushing
the engine of the ribs with its heart like a motor,
to see the world end   in your room among
the stood-up knives
Your belly dogged by alcohol
Your frivolous heart-beat, out of time,
armslength from any   other

It pushes you like a sore friend
into the stopped windows of your body
Where you drink until the dream   shuts its face
& goes away
Until, amid the spill of nightfall,
you stagger freely,
the fantastic world's end   squeezing your bones

Tricks

for Trix, a dog

This is a life in which
a case of whisky is one drink.
In it, a dog goes totally blind & no one knows
if it remembers its young doghood,
the smell of wild mountains carried in storm
from the high passes

I feel I am in the world & there is no god in it with me.
These days my husband gets up & sits
on the edge of our bed & says
a case of whisky is one drink.
He says there are glasses as big as women filled with rye &
                                                    he wants
to marry one.
This is what I listen to, no wonder
I can't sleep.
Faintly
I hear the heart-tick of my old dog in Calgary, 800 miles away.
She sleeps on the porch, & shies away when the footsteps
come, crying gently.
When there are no footfalls, she rests & waits to die.

I want to leave my husband & let him marry
all the bottles in Vancouver,
while I go to Calgary to sit beside the blind dog of the family,
her eyes muddy with cataract,
& tell her of her old/young doghood, of hikes to the ice-caves
with a black pup in '71, who was herself
splay-legged on the fireroad.
I want to tell her she is a dog who loved the mountains,
& she should be proud even in blindness
that she saw them & climbed their hard trails,
& camped there with the humans
like a god.
Now she is only afraid, of being stepped on.
She knows our voices, even mine that she hears so seldom.
She speaks back in her small voice
& snuffles nearer.
I wish she would remember & be proud, but she lives
only the present in her dogged blind way,
fighting the back stairs.

Without her memories I am alone in the world, the god gone
                                          out of it.
My husband murmurs over, *the root is still there,*
in the whole world there is only whisky for one drink.
No wonder I can't sleep.
No wonder to look at the world is to go blind in it

Proceedings of the Wars

Randy winds up his sayings into a knot, sufficient to live by.
John pulls them out & unwinds them.
Paul stares at me, the same far-off
anger of my father forty years ago, the neat hair.
I start to fall in love with stones.

My friends are turning grey without recourse.
They've stopped talking of civilization & the slums.
This is what it's come to.

Together we drive cars we never intended, & live
in houses, essay to be ordinary.
Our children surround us like flags.
We teach them what our fathers knew, thinking it honest.
Together we converse & the old revolts are
shaken into rows, laughable, curious, depleted as
mod clothes.
Our lives diminished, *real* we say.

So I've stopped drinking, content with *a high lifetime average.*
What I crave
in particular, the sun at 5 am, a glass
of cold water, I watch the birds pick the yard up in their beaks
& set it down.

A life of friendship every six months renewed.
The old touch made strange, our talk
more & more polite.

The generation we were, wanting to change all this,
wanting to end:
Now it is our own backs
turning from the young with their rough music,
the harshness of *Nuke the Suburbs*.

We are the parade of ourselves, maudlin & alive like ticks
in houses.
Our well-spent paycheques clutter us.
Like my father forty years past, we are sensible & articulate.
The planet is orderly.
Our lives, circle the building in which we are champion;
they labour to find an entrance without stairs

Professional Amnesia

He remembers family reunions at Lake Somewhere, each summer
the women running toward the water
laughing,
holding eggs in spoons
In his memory they keep on running,
he can't remember when they reach the water,
their clothes streaked with sand & grass
Or is it
the target shoots he claims had happened,
shooting at old records, ribbons, plastic soldiers
thrown up by the other children,
his cousins, who never grew

In his memory the women are still running,
the water does not rise to meet them,
they run right out of his life
so their names are forgotten
Family names
Family memories, the accusations one parent made
against the other
while he sat outside, his head
pressed against the cold tree that shaded his room

He remembers who stayed away each Christmas but not who came,
who wouldn't cut the turkey,
who stood up in shirt & tie & armbands
& sharpened knives against the steel.
The eaters are forgotten, the celebrations spontaneous
combustions;
when he speaks of family
the women are running out of it, into a summer lake of air

Doe-Face

Soft fur of her doe-face in the snow below the rails
Brown on brown body, warm-blooded, still
The cow elk hears the ticking of
her hunger
The animals of prey do not attack her
Know she will die here & they will eat from her
Easy meat
Hit by the passenger train, skidded down
the snow slope into silence
Wild she gazes, soft ears spread out, supplicant among trees
her body alert as the trains speed above
Their track so civilized & named
A siding called Palliser, below it
the elk waits, grass torn from beneath the snow
as far as she could nuzzle,
unable to stand
Already she does not know what her life was, she
becomes the snow, lain in trees under the mountain

It's our emotion, not hers
She doesn't feel the heart welling up
or know she waits to die
That's just us, projecting our own incapacity,
her body still alive
suffering pain without cry or madness
She looks up, her long ears & animal intensity,
legs folded under her,
a brown patch in the white sentence
She watches our train pass,
without coming down from our dangerous track
to know & rescue her from hunger
To touch her
Bringing in our arms, like game wardens,
a warm shot for her

Post-Modern Literature

Less to insist upon, fewer
proofs.
Raw metals pulled from the ground, cheaply.
Or a woman in the televised film shouting: thanks to you
I end up surrounded by violence.
So much gratitude, Saturday nights spent
believing in it.

But the end of a city is still
a field, ordinary persons live there, a frame house, & occasionally—
a woman comes out to hang the washing.
From a certain angle you see her
push a line of wet clothes across a suburb.
It sings in the wind there, against
stucco, lilacs, sunken front porches, windows
where nobody moves.
But carefully.   All of it

made carefully, children in snowsuits
after school, appear in the doorway, carry
their tracks shyly.
& you at the kitchen table—your empty
bowl streaked by the spoon, the meal's
memory, papers, juice in one glass, whisky
in another, unwritten greeting cards,
a watch, applesauce, small white medallions.

As if saying the name fixes.
As if the woman will come out again, & pull down
an entire suburb with her washing.
As if the city *could* end, in a field or
anywhere.
or if the woman on the bright TV could
stop saying *thank you.*
or you, saying "like this", & pointing shyly.
Too much paper, the children
in their snowsuits holding doorways, white snow,
parrots, singing smuggled information, the corporation gone to

Guatemala.
Leaving Father, the curling rink, a woman dressed
in grey parka & the nearest boots pulling
stiff clothes away from the weather, the back road, post-modern
                                        literature

ben soo

Ken Norris

[You are reading this too fast.]

You are reading this too fast.
Slow down, for this is poetry
and poetry works slowly.
Unless you live with it a while
the spirit will never descend.
It's so easy to quickly cut across the surface
and then claim there was nothing to find.
Touch the poem gently with your eyes
just as you would touch a lover's flesh.
Poetry is an exercise in patience,
you must wait for it to come to you.
The spirit manifests in many guises;
some quiver with beauty,
some vibrate with song.
What is happening?
Slow down, slow down,
take a few deep breaths,
read the poem slowly,
read the lines one at a time,
read the words one by one,
read the spaces between the words,
get sleepy, this is poetry,
relax until your heart
is vulnerable, wide open.

The Trouble with Angels

The trouble with angels
Is that they buckle at the waist,
Bellies overlapping where their genitals
Should be. The trouble is that
They've always got an eye on the clock,
Are always reckoning the time till Judgement Day.
The trouble is their wings won't lie
Flat on the bed once we've gotten them
That far; the trouble is that, by
Necessity, they have to be on top.
The trouble is the insane desire we feel
To pluck their wings feather by feather.
The trouble is that by day they look so lovely
But glowing in the dark by night so frightening.
The trouble with angels is that the world
Has provided no place for them.

In Pursuit of Love

Chasing you down the street, you are walking & I am running & still I get no closer, knocking myself out over you, it's been twenty-three miles of this, & I am crying, a face full of tears, & you are walking slowly but deliberately step after step into the time of your life.

Chasing you around the bed all night long, & you in retreat though you tell me it's love, & I keep after you to the four corners of the bed where I fall upon you & start you heading for another point of the compass.

Chasing you, calling you by the thousand names of love, calling you perfection & knowing I am lying, calling you on the phone, asking if I can come home yet, asking, always asking, though never pleading, though maybe once, always asking you to love me.

Chasing you in a fast car, make it a Maserati, & you in your English elegance, driving fast ahead of me in a compact convertible, your hand on the stick shift, every time you shift gears I can feel my heart failing, but driving on in pursuit, knowing I can't do anything but try, knowing we may pile up around any turn, cruising by any tree, not caring, putting my hand on the wheel & heading straight for that big oak, you wrenching the wheel back & slamming on the brakes, yelling at me for wanting to kill you when it's really the both of us that I want to kill.

Chasing you through the streets of New York, buying you a drink at every bar, trying to rein you in, trying to follow you down, following you down & then waking up to find you gone, chasing you a thousand times like Apollo after the sweet sweet ass of Daphne, how many times you magically get turned into a tree & I stroke your bark & try to call you out, but you are wood, frozen between earth & sky.

Chasing you & then catching you, & you toss me up into the air & catch me & toss me again & again & again & there are rivers flowing where we lie, & then you lie to me again & again & again.

Chasing you, an angel, up through the celestial sphere, trying to clip the wings of your purity, trying to drag you, in your white robes, down into some muddy bed, stepping on clouds, trying to get to you, & hating you for every step you make me take up & away from the earth, wanting very little of your spirituality, but wanting your body lightly dusted by it, & being tied by my own handicaps, & being tied by the other angels that hover all around you, & being tired of the mystic rose you wear in your hair.

The Case

for J.

I waited long into the night for you to call me,
playing detective with the stars trying to solve
the greater mystery, while you danced off
somewhere in the distance, mysterious as always.
There is a man with a key, and there is
the man who locks you out of doors.
I wander through the night in my trenchcoat
trying to stop thinking about a taste of you,
the desire for it that makes all good guys turn bad.

Sleep solves the case as always, and dream,
well dream gives us reasons
to kill and lie and cheat, dream leads
to a life of crime, and you lead me
out and away from all the integrities
until I too begin chasing falcons and start forgetting
about bodies buried shallowly in lakes.

A Short Treatise Upon Our Failures

We fail. Often. It is as if
there can be no reprieve from it;
a sentence pronounced. Like trees
unable to bear fruit. When we say
we are working it out we mean
we are trying to understand where it went wrong.
It was a spring evening, or early one morning.

& so we go on, often wondering why
we go on, but given no choice now
of doing much else. We say "It looks
like rain," prepare ourselves for a day of it.

2.

We fail. To explain the limits
& so there is strife. A natural battle,
really. You say this is more
than you bargained for & I don't understand.
We wind up at the border stations of the world
held for questioning. Occasionally they search.
We wonder what they are looking for. It is
nothing unusual, a stick of this or that.
Yet there is violation; if only we could
have spoken of it more clearly.

3.

We fail. It is a winter morning
& there is no sense in getting up.
Yet to lie in bed is to admit defeat:
the last great crime. Behind us
the red carpet of sleep has been rolled away.
Ahead there is only vacuous space
stretching out for as many miles as we can walk.
There is no sense in that; we must give up
the notion of walking. There must be
something else. Silence. Someone else?

Ode to the Day

These hours of light,
we awaken to them, cling to them;
working our ways through timed routines
we so often wonder where they go,
they are the visible life.
Journeying through the hours
we glimpse the world, the cities,
we almost face the light unflinchingly
and call what we face 'day'.

But 'the day' is a fullness,
the endless wedding of light & dark,
a perfecting act of balance.
The world turns our eyes to the sun
then turns them to the stars,
we see a blazing fire
encircled by airy blue, we see smaller fires
encased in dark, and with them in the night sky
a moon, telling of another nature.

All this is the day:
the waking & the working & the sleeping,
the loving, the despairs,
our lives travelling a circling course,
our bodies encountering the air,
the earth, the beautiful machinery,
our minds filling up with tidal pools of reality
and the half-lit bounty of dreams,
our hearts beating strongly for the eternity of a day
as the world turns once and we manage it,
only rarely getting dizzy.

Here/There

for Daphne & Endre & Claudia

Here there are the red hibiscus flowers that come reaching
                                        into the heart,
there is rain and a reign of terror that spreads out from the fronds
                                        of the high palms,
the world dreams in terror of awakening to a day when everything
                                        is possible
and no choice can be made. Rooster crows, I have seen him
                                        strutting and crowing
in three countries spread across so much ocean between.
Between us there are thousands of miles, thousands of dreams,
we reach inside each other sometimes to pull out a bouquet
                                        of roses
to tempt the hearts of strangers with, the heart knows
far too much for its own good, there are illnesses, sicknesses
of the heart that will never end, we call one desire,
call another want, we call another love and stand in the hallways
                                        of hospitals
trying to contract it, we stand in the sunlight and our arms
are around each other if only we weren't so shy.

Here the rain has stopped and it is a green day, as the days
are always green now with growth and a jealousy
that's bred out of the heart's darker nature, longing for
                                        everything
that this is not. A world exists, this is not the world,
only a small part of it that once was foreign, alien, and now
is the terrain of everyday life. The human mind is green with
                                        jadedness,
the tikis were seen in a land that was passed through, a love
was contracted and some greenstone given, across ocean,
                                        across time

held for a moment in the arms of a person once a stranger,
then familiar, then almost known, her response revealed,
a certain movement making her tremble, the insistence
                                              of knowledge.

"Can I say I love you?" she asks in a cabin by a lake,
discovering for the first time how it is done that way,
for the first time the emotional part of it revealed to me.
"Yes," I can only say, "you are free to say what you feel,
this is a foreign country, there is no need for further disguises,
we do not recognize the landscape and the landscape does not
                                              recognize us.
What we recognize is there, not here, I do not
recognize you, have we met before, before we came
to be here in one another's arms? Will I recognize you
there if we should meet again, will we shed our clothes
and meet again at the center of desire?
When we leave, will we go on living in this cabin,
replicas spun out from us to inhabit the world
we are knowing now?" There is silence and darkness,
the silence and darkness of the unknown as stars burn bright
in the Southern Sky, we walk beneath it, constellations unfamiliar,
there is my old friend Orion, and there the Southern Cross,
there is the part that has somehow come to meet me here,
there is the part that is different and strange;
we are looking at the sky and it is not the sky,
it is something created in the image of the sky we have known,
someone has reshaped the heavens, we hold hands
and I want to run away to where I once was.

There I imagine the roses came to rest on the night table
beside her bed, arriving with such surprise, she opens
the door and a stranger is handing her flowers, it is winter,

do I need to suggest snow has fallen, it is
winter, that time of purity, and snow
has fallen upon the wrapping that swaddles those red red roses,
symbol of desiring love I knew I was sending her;
and flowers too, flowers of course, the thing is only ever itself
though we may desire all association, the thing
stripped down to its essence, as she once shed her clothes,
as her long hair once fell lightly in the springtime of our
nakedness.
The flowers arrive and fill the room, and then slowly,
                              with the days,
they begin to fill her heart.

There the snow is falling for the last time, and then
the slow, freeing process of the thaw begins,
lovers walk in mud and then they walk upon grass,
there will be flowers raising their eyes to the sun,
sunlight falling on newly washed cars, the grime
of a long, grueling season cleared away. A cross
is reaching for the sky, across the road a soccer ball flies
                              between teams,
the city is alive again, the city is dirty
and busy and bustling with all of that confused life,
that purposelessness working itself towards different ends.
We dream of an end and produce the means, this we call
the way we live, living such an open-formed thing, a petalled thing,
this is the structure of our lives I say opening and closing my hand,
as the heart opens and closes pumping blood, allowing love,
we are feverish with the alternation, as our lives,
as our lovers walk slowly towards us across a sun-dappled room.

Cook Islands

Monty Reid

The Road Back and Forth to Ryley

The mist splits open for light the way the heart
is parted for clarity. On the fields
at the edge of town white-tail browse
dark air damp on their pelage. Morning
edges down the road behind us and we've
forgotten the camera, as we always do when
deer are there, but always have it when dead skunks
and porcupines lie on the shoulders, entrails
plucked by magpies, ravens, unphotogenic crows.
Or we're late for work and can't stop.
The deer lift their heads but don't run
and the ground goes fluent with dawn.

Or the dark in mid-winter.
Through the moraine at Cooking Lake
where glaciers off the mountains and the shield
met and ground slowly into one another.
Now the snow through aspens that cover
the hummocks of till. Cones of light.
Drifts climb from the ditches, sprawl
unself-consciously over the road and we follow
the snowplow at thirty mph not
seeing anything except the blue light
diffract in white.

The girls they have for flagmen wave you down.
Euclids belly along the roadbed, the dirt
all ruts or hung in the air like an allergy
and it's summer, the girls in hardhats and
haltertops, shoulders flushed with
sun. All you can see is dust. Or farther
past the construction, where heat wraps the highway
in cellophane, the way things are packaged
so you don't see what you've got til you've paid
for it. But I could drive this road
blindfolded.

The city hoists itself into light
block by block on threads of smoke
and the traffic thickens, bumper to bumper
all the way in from Sherwood Park and when one stops
everybody does. If you were with me
you'd be nervous, stiffening every time
someone merged ahead of us, your foot
pumps an imaginary brake.
                                        At night, from Ryley
the city's glare floats on the horizon like the nest
of a waterbird. In the morning, driving,
it disappears.

Test Drive
(*for Jack and Leona*)

It's spring, the roads
full of frost heaves and pot-holes
but you don't feel them. The shocks
compress. In the backseat
the salesman holds on to the armrest
and winces. There's a lot
of protection there in case you have
an accident he says; the clouds
reflect in the long hood. It feels
like you're riding on air. Through
the sunroof we watch the high flights
of Canada geese drift through their
flyways. We explore the electric
windows and remote-control mirrors
and barely notice the image: ducks
that nest at the roadside launched
into the air. A stupid panic
when we drive so noiselessly
by.

Her Story

I was born in a hospital in a small town
     beside a large shallow lake. My mother
said while she lay there, between the spasms of
     pain, she could hear the hard
flights of mallard and pintail, avocets, bittern
     heron, the ragged v's of Canada geese
come flailing in to the mudflats and reed beds
     around the lake. When I cried they may have
heard me there, the birds gathering on the shore
     before migration.

Once I had appendicitis and there were no birds
     but once, when I was getting my tonsils
out, I lay propped up on the pillows and watched
     the gulls, herring and ring-billed and California
even a glaucous, strut around the incinerator
     pecking at scraps of garbage
generals plotting a coup.

Later, my eldest son being born
     prematurely into the world and the birds
were there then. In fact, we had been out hunting
     and it may have been the squatting in the cold
blind while the mist came off the lake like a wool
     sweater, the steel of the shotgun ice
against my cheek, that brought the birth
     on early. Or it may have been the excitement, the gun
bruising my shoulder, the weight of ducks
     we carried back to the truck, or it may simply
have been the smallness of my body and its inability
     to carry full term. But he was early.
We weren't sure he would live. And the birds
     were there then too. I dreamt them tumbling
shot out of the sky above the hospital.

I live now near the lake I was born beside.
    The kids aren't that interested in birds.
I watch the herons and cranes and storks
    flap over and my husband yells at the gulls
that shit on the fence he's just painted.
    I sometimes think the birds are crazy
to keep coming back to this lake
    tho I love watching them
and I also know
    they can't help it.

Spring Ease

In March the waxwings picked the shrivelled berries
off the ash tree. The cat twitched at the window
and the grey clouds edged under the horizon.
Slow month. Now the birds turn on the wind
that whips the clouds from the sky, the cat
scratches at the door. The girl, whose eyes
also are grey, who says the kitchen's hot,
lets the cat out as she herself leaves for a walk
among the hills, hunting for crocus. April.
May. The boys work overtime. She sits on the hill's
south face, a flower in her hand.
Now there is only desire, warm
ground. Her eyes follow the cloud over
the hills. Sun and wind flush her face
as love would. In the kitchen she sets the plates
on the tablecloth covered with flowers.
The men come in from the field
and don't notice.

The Shorebirds

Snowy owls still sit on the ice in the middle
of the lake, quiet as the arctic all afternoon
and in the evening hunt along the shore.
A muskrat pushes angles through the ring
of open water and among the cattails
dried out by winter a blackbird caws.
And I would have thought it too early
for geese but they spill out of their corners
in the sky and slap into the water. When
I come back the next day the owls are gone.

It starts that way: with disappearance.
The wrist of ice melts from the ring of
black water; bracelet swallows bone.
We stand on the soggy hummocks with cameras
and binoculars around our necks, watch
flights land on the flooded meadows,
the cold lake. These migrants
full of distance: snipe, plover,
whimbrel. They fill this empty
season with their noise.

Sometimes I think they don't trust the water,
these birds that live on the lake-edge.
Why else the long legs, the herons
four feet above the surface, drawn up
to protect a dignity that survives even
the frogs they pluck from grass blades.
Or the godwits on one leg like kids
with bootfulls. We watch from a blind
stitched together from reeds and bulrush
and mare's tail, tell ourselves the birds
don't see us, don't mind us here.

Needle beaks. The avocets pluck
midges off the mudflats. Parliaments
of knots and sandpipers legislate along
the margins of the lake. They vote
bugs into their mouths. Egrets from California.
Sometimes you see a banded leg, the capture
carried there like jewellery. We write
on them and try to set them free
and fail. Out of season, we watch
an owl, gone brown in the chest
drift soundlessly north.

Rock Tumbler

In the porch
small barrels turn
over and over
with pebbles in them.
The grit
wears the stone
down. Moon rocks
from India, agates,
they revolve
and fall, revolve
and fall, and
the edges disintegrate.
The kids have already
lost the cheap settings
the stones were to be
glued to: tie-clips,
rings. The instructions
said tumbling was just
like stream action
only speeded up.
The barrels turn all
night and I can hear
a river scraping
through the house.
A woman
fishes in the water
for a stone.

Tractor Hour

Pat found the station the last time she
came out here. Driving home alone after dropping
the kids off, suitcases and a bagful of patching,
she said she wasn't used to the quiet. Around her
in the fields she could see the big four-wheel
drives unreel the earth behind them. Deep tillage.
They drag the heart up to the surface.
Behind her the highway stretched out like summerfallow.

And on the radio, turning the needle
back and forth past the local country
station and talkshows, the bible hour, past
the voices that fade in and out, overlapping.
What goes on in the air is so erratic.
She found the Tractor Hour, the dj taking
calls and dedicating songs to the guys out
in the cabs, talking fertilizer, wheat board,
machinery. The calls came in: "I'd like to
dedicate something by Waylon Jennings to my dad
who's out doing summerfallow on Hetland's old
quarter," or "Could you play Don't It Make my Brown
Eyes Blue for Don who's driving the Co-op bulk
truck today?" And every now and then, Pat could see
someone high in a cab with a set of headphones on.

She held the needle on that station until she
couldn't hear it any more. It went the way jeans
go, something showing through that looks like skin
and bone. Sometimes they're not worth fixing.
But a month later when we went to pick the kids
up, they were waiting for us, excited because Tom
let them drive his tractor and it even had a radio
and Grandma got the radio to play a song for them.
And David ripped his pants climbing into a steel
bin and Grandma had to sew them.

Driving home the next day
we listened to the Tractor Hour again
the car full of the usual human noise,
the radio's needle patching the sound
over us so that all we can do is look
at each other and hum the music
that's there.

Robyn Sarah

Maintenance

Sometimes the best I can do
is homemade soup, or a patch on the knee
of the baby's overalls.
Things you couldn't call poems.
Things that spread in the head,
that swallow
whole afternoons, weigh down the week
till the elastic's gone right out of it—
so gone
it doesn't even snap when it breaks.
And one spent week's
just like the shapeless bag
of another. Monthsful of them,
with new ones rolling in and
filling up with the same junk: toys
under the bed, eggplant slices sweating
on the breadboard, the washing machine
spewing suds into the toilet, socks
drying on the radiator and falling down
behind it where the dust lies furry and
full of itself . . . The dust!
what I could tell you about
the dust. How it eats things—
pencils, caps from ballpoint pens,
plastic sheep, alphabet blocks.
How it spins cocoons
around them, clumps up and
smothers whatever strays into
its reaches—buttons,
pennies, marbles—and then

how it lifts, all of a piece,
dust-pelts
thick as the best velvet
on the bottom of the mop.
                                        Sometimes
the best that I can do
is maintenance: the eaten
replaced by the soon-to-be-eaten, the raw
by the cooked, the spilled-on
by the washed and dried, the ripped
by the mended; empty cartons
heaved down the cellar stairs, the
cans stacked on the ledge, debris
sealed up in monstrous snot-green bags
for the garbage man.

And I'll tell you what
they don't usually tell you: there's no
poetry in it. There's no poetry
in scraping concrete off the high chair tray
with a bent kitchen knife, or fishing
with broomhandle behind the fridge
for a lodged ball. None in the sink
that's always full, concealing its cargo
of crockery under a head
of greasy suds. Maybe you've heard
that there are compensations? That, too's
a myth. It doesn't work that way.
The planes are separate. Even if there are
moments each day that take you by the heart
and shake the dance back into it, that you lost
the beat of, somewhere years behind—even if
in the clear eye of such a moment you catch
a glimpse of the only thing worth looking for—
to call this compensation, is to demean.

The planes are separate. And it's the
other one, the one called maintenance,
I mostly am shouting about.
I mean the day-to-day,
that bogs the mind, voice, hands
with things you couldn't call poems.
I mean the thread that breaks.
The dust between
typewriter keys.

Cat's Cradle

When women together sit sipping
cold tea and tugging at the
threads of memory, thoughtfully
pulling at this
or that bit or loop, or slipping
this loop over that finger till
warp and weft of past lives begin
crazily to unwind, when women sit
smoking and talking, the talk
making smoke in the air, when they shake
shreds of tobacco out of a crumpled pack
and keep drinking the same weak tea
from the same broken pot, something clicks
in the springs of the clock
and it's yesterday again,
and the sprung yarn rolls down loose
from the spool of the moon.

When women together sit talking
an afternoon, when they talk
the sun down, talk stars, talk
dawn—they talk up a dust
of sleeping dogs and bones
and they talk a drum for the dust
to dance to, till the dance
drums up a storm; when women
sit drumming fingers on tops
of tables, when the tables turn
into tops that spin and hum
and the bobbin of the moon
keeps spinning its fine yarn down
to catch fingers, when fingers catch
talk in a cat's cradle, and turn
talk into a net to catch the curve
of the storm—then it's talk
against talk, till the tail
of the storm trails into dust
and they talk the dust back down.

Things that matter and don't matter
are caught together, things done and undone,
and the kettle boils dry and over
while they lean closer to peer down
into the murky water where last night's dream
flicks its tail and is gone
(and the reel of the moon keeps cranking
its long line down), when women together
sit sipping cold tea and sawing on the strings
of memory, it is an old tune.
The rice sticks to the bottom of the pan
and things get left out in the rain.

An Inch of Air

She wants to talk, but he
won't have it—talk—just circular
and besides, he's tired. He flicks
the lamp off, making
an end of it. And there they lie
like two cats, back to back,
in a bed too small for them.
In a moment he's under, a boy chasing
apples down a slope, some other boy
launching them down from a tree. But she,
eyes open in the dark, nerves wired,
writhes like a hooked fish on the line
of his breathing—strung in mid-air
till morning, with a quarrel to revive
over breakfast—what kind of a life. She gives
the sheets a yank—they're caught
under him—another tug
frees them, and he snores on,
uncovered. She curls up
like a spring, timed to uncoil
with the first light. And moves
an inch over, to put some token air
between her back and his.

An Early Start in Mid-Winter

The freeze is on. At six a scattering
of sickly lights shine pale in kitchen windows.
Thermostats are adjusted. Furnaces
blast on with a whoosh. And day
rumbles up out of cellars to the tune
of bacon spitting in a greasy pan.

Scrape your nail along the window-pane,
shave off a curl of frost. Or press your thumb
against the film of white to melt an eye
onto the fire escape. All night
pipes ticked and grumbled like sore bones.
The tap runs rust over your chapped hands.

Sweep last night's toast-crumbs off the tablecloth.
Puncture your egg-yolk with a prong of fork
so gold runs over the white. And sip
your coffee scalding hot. The radio
says you are out ahead, with time to spare.
Your clothes are waiting folded on the chair.

This is your hour to dream. The radio
says that the freeze is on, and may go on
weeks without end. You barely hear the warning.
Dreaming of orange and red, the hot-tongued flowers
that winter sunrise mimics, you go out
in the dark. And zero floats you into morning.

Broom At Twilight

Some climbs end nowhere. Like the unplanned climb
I took this evening.
                 I'd gone down the beach
some little way, and though the sun was low,
I thought that it would see me round those rocks
to the next cove, with time enough to watch
the tide come in (and maybe make it back
without getting my feet wet.)
                    No such luck—
beyond that stretch, the tide was in already,
and there was nothing to do but climb the cliffs
up to the road, and walk back home that way.

Dark doesn't wait, this time of year. I climbed,
and the sun went down as I went up. Went right on
falling beyond the unseen edge faster
than I could find my holds. (Footholds in clay,
handholds on anchored roots. And all the while
the sky fast darkening out from above.)

               Near water,
the grey hour's luminous. And by the beach
I should have had no trouble finding my way.
Where I came up, though—something blocked the light.
It was the sameness that surprised me.

Broom:
a forest of it. Higher than my head.
And not in clumps, the way it seems to grow
by day—but in a solid wall. An army
bristling with strange intent. The broom I knew
grew in tall waving tufts like uncut hay
to wade through at high noon. This broom stood up
like earth's raised hackles in the failing light—
a massing of ominous spikes against the sky
and stems that wouldn't give way. I couldn't find
the mouse-paths children make to get to the sea—
but had to plunge (broom closing over me)
into a tangible edgeless element,
banking on where I thought the road must be.

Suckers for Truth

How much longer do you suppose
we can get away with it, edging
a little closer to the fire, sitting up
long past midnight, stubborn holdouts
in the unseasonable cold? The effects
of too much wine, of wine at the wrong time
have begun to take their toll, dredging up moments
that had gone unnoticed, but return now
to trouble us, like a funny noise
in the engine, that we register gradually
but manage to avoid talking about for miles

The landscape falls away
on either side of us, some of the trees
already turning, far ahead a darkening
as yet more felt than seen, seeming to indicate
we're heading into a storm front
and we don't care, do we, switching the radio
to another station, watching the signs
for a roadside diner, somewhere to unzip
and grab a sandwich, coffees to take out,
while we congratulate ourselves
for making good time

It's not as though we aren't aware
of the pitfalls, but that we know
procrastination is our best defense,
so far we have not committed ourselves
and it shows, there's that comfortable rubble
on the seats and floor we'd have to clear away
to get down to business, oddly festive
and a bit risqué, till now it has seemed
easiest to tack strips of old carpeting
over the cracks, when the thing falls apart
we're hoping it will do it all at once

A camp stool, a tin pot, and an old
umbrella, stage props for a stay
against confusion, we find ways
to laugh at the rain, and in it,
and to accommodate our guests, so much
depends on the things glimpsed
in the rear-view mirror, wheelbarrows
and such, it seems that with luck
a kind of courtship happens between the lines
and it's this we're after: without the risk
what would be possible?

Sharon Thesen

From *Parts of Speech: 12 Poems*

5. Usage

Do not read these words.
There are too many words written
already. It's all been
said before, everyone knows that.
There are 31 stories, or 29, or 42,
everything is the same old story.
All you have to do is
pick up your daily newspaper
& there they are,
the same old stories.
Words everywhere. A trillion
trillion words laid end to end
would stretch around the globe
a hundred times. Equators
of words, ropes
tying the world up tight,
creasing the oceans & strangling you
in your bed at night.
Dear reader, take heed &
by the way,
will you marry me?

7. The Argument Begins with A

Love,
whoever do you
resemble.
Not a snake,
not a thing
in the dark.
Your appearance
brings dread to the heart,
knowledge
unasked for.
In the lamplight
your eyes are green
your inevitable wound
is red. A brown moth
pins herself
against the wall,
her wings are hers
unwished for.
Wing & heart
—slide toward each other
along a trajectory
called love, exchange
for a moment,
their properties. A wing-shaped
heart. A heart-shaped
wing. A beating stillness. A
motionless weight.

12. The End

The body
is a transparency
of desire

to be seen
a mass
of contradictions

holding flesh to bone
moon to fingernail

to be seen
for itself alone, its
preciseness
eyes look out of
seeing the
being seen
it wants

There was that time
I saw you looking at me

through the back door window
& the door was locked
& I turned on my feet
so the gauzy nightgown swirled
around

& you could hardly bear
how much you wanted in

Mean Drunk Poem

Backward & down into inbetween as Vicki says. Or as Robin teaches
the gap, from which all things emerge. A left
handed compliment. Bats, houses of parliament, giants, stones.
What woman, witness to such Thought, does not feel
so described & so impotent

she thinks
she must speak. 'I will take your linguistic prick & you
will take my linguistic prick & together we will gap
this imagined earth together.' She has the feeling,
all her life, that she never makes sense. There is something
else, big & dark, at the edge of what she knows, she cannot
say. She always has the feeling she is translating into
Broken english. Language all her life is a second language,
the first is mute & exists. I get drunk

to lubricate my brain & all that comes out
of my Gap
is more bloody writing. No wonder we cook dinner. Have another
kid. Write poetry about the Beloved & kiss ass.
Who cares, as Eleanor says,
who beats whose door down yelling Truth.

The door is only &
always an entrance.

Sing Om as you take the sausage rolls out of the oven.
The Gap is real & there is no such thing as
female intelligence. We're dumber than hell.

Loose Woman Poem

for Victoria Walker & Penny Kemp

A landscape
full of holes.
Women.
Pierced
ears voices piercing
the ceiling, a little choir
stung by wine:
I Fall to Pieces, and
Please Release Me.
After which I put on my old wedding band
& go to the party.
Next day 222's
& the moon falls out
of my fingernail.
The house smells like oysters
& a moon is on the loose
a woman in the bathtub   another
talking on the phone, their presence
shimmers, I'm fed up
with the wages of sin
put on some Mingus
& hepcat around

how come
it's always a question
of loss, being sick of self
displaced & frantic, chopped out
of the World of Discourse
waylaid
on the Bridge of Sighs, a net
work of connections coming down
to getting laid
or not getting laid & by whom.
Except getting laid
is not the way she thinks of it,
more like
something that her moons
can waylay waylay waylay
in the dark.

Discourse

A quiet night, they all are.
My kid asleep
my husband out screwing around
the cat also. Even spring
is false, crocuses sprout purple
into January sunlight,
poor little things.

Outside, at a glance
headlights dance in the alleyway
mercury vapor night entranced

Women laughing somewhere
dogs barking, Susie splitting up
with Tom at Bino's Pancake House.

And finally there's not
all that much
you can say.

The small vocabulary
of love needs its own
thin blue dictionary.

Praxis

Unable to imagine a future,
imagine a future better
than now, us creatures
weeping *in the abattoir*
only make noise & do
not transform a single fact.
So stop crying. Get up. Go out. Leap
the mossy garden wall
the steel fence or whatever
the case may be & crash
through painted arcadias,
fragments of bliss & roses
decorating your fists.

Lecture Noir

Where there is silence
suddenly, as if you
had expected it.
Starts out with
nothing clear
nothing false.

The world enters
weeping—I see a poet
in an old hotel
drunk with a blue
ballpoint pen
over his ear, dreary
periwinkle of all our hours
pinched & blackened
at the edges—
roses, windows
& dread. You thinketh
this sentiment
too fancy, eh,
a 19th Century style (anguish
bothers the dead.) Baudelaire's
self-introduction:
je suis poète,
alcoolique, pédéraste.
And then, the black stream
of countered words.
Crimson gladiolus
in a shop window
nearly brings me to tears—
call the poet
a love poet
then watch her hands—
you'd be surprised
what she does
with the roses.

Hello Goodbye

The quiet of a silver afternoon
quickens, a magnet scattering
of books under lampshades
& in the gentle, eerie music
the skyline of Toronto. Helpless,
I yearn for this one or that one
happy in their houses or unhappy
as the case may be. This wasn't
supposed to happen, yet I miss
you all. The music holds me

& won't let go. I grow small,
diminished by all the goodnatured
goodbyes, the 747's taking off,
the daily effort to solve
the puzzled heart. I miss you all
& believe and don't believe
the twisted appearance of completion
as things keep ending. The music

remembers. It hath a soft
& dying fall. God knows
the sentimental beast has spoken
& I wish you were here
anyway. In the lateness
of it all enchantment is not
a dim luxury surrounded by fools.
In the lateness of it all
a numbing silence & the rhythm
of another word written,
and another.

Notes on the Authors

Born in 1952, ROO BORSON has lived and worked at a variety of non-literary jobs in Vancouver and Toronto. In 1977 she completed an M.F.A. in creative writing at the University of British Columbia. In 1982 she won first prize for poetry in the CBC Literary Competition.

Books: *Landfall,* 1977
  In the Smoky Light of the Fields, 1980
  Rain, 1980
  Night Walk, 1981
  A Sad Device, 1981
  The Whole Night, Coming Home, 1984

MARILYN BOWERING was born in Winnipeg (1949) and brought up in Victoria, B.C. She has lived and worked in Canada, the United States, Greece and Scotland in film, radio, marketing and communications, and as an editor and teacher. She currently lives in Sooke, B.C. and teaches in the Department of Creative Writing at the University of Victoria.

Books: *The Liberation of Newfoundland,* 1973
  One Who Became Lost, 1976
  The Killing Room, 1977
  Third Child/Zian, 1978
  The Book of Glass, 1979
  The Visitors Have All Returned, 1979
  Sleeping With Lambs, 1980
  Giving Back Diamonds, 1982
  The Sunday Before Winter: New and Selected Poems, 1984

LORNA CROZIER has taught creative writing at the Saskatchewan Summer School of the Arts for several years. Her most recent book, *The Weather*, and also *Crow's Black Joy* were winners in the Saskatchewan Writers' Guild poetry competitions. She has been a recipient of the Saskatchewan Arts' Board Senior Artists' Award and will be writer-in-residence at the Regina Public Library for 1984-1985.

Books: *Inside Is the Sky*, 1976
       Crow's Black Joy, 1978
       No Longer Two People, 1979
       Humans and Other Beasts, 1980
       The Weather, 1983

BARRY DEMPSTER was born and raised in Toronto. He was educated in child psychology and has worked at both the Children's Aid and the Lakeshore Psychiatric Hospital. His first book of poetry, *Fables for Isolated Men* (1982), was a finalist for the Governor-General's Award. He is presently reviews editor for *Poetry Canada Review*.

Books: *Third Impressions* (with Don Dickinson
          and Dave Margoshes), 1982
       Fables for Isolated Men, 1982
       Globe Doubts, 1983
       Real Places and Imaginary Men, 1984
       David and the Daydreams, 1984

CHRISTOPHER DEWDNEY was born in London, Ontario in 1951. He has published and exhibited internationally, and his work has stirred excitement in England and the United States as well as Canada. He lives in Toronto, where he teaches Coeval Literature at York University.

Books: *Golders Green,* 1972
        A Paleozoic Geology of London, Ontario, 1973
        Fovea Centralis, 1975
        Spring Trances in the Control Emerald Night, 1978
        Alter Sublime, 1980
        Spring Trances in the Control Emerald Night/The Cenozoic Asylum, 1982
        Predators of the Adoration: Selected Poems 1972-82, 1983

Born in 1949 in Arezzo, Italy, PIER GIORGIO DI CICCO was raised in Montreal, Baltimore and Toronto. In 1973 he graduated from the University of Toronto (B.A., B. Ed.). His poems have appeared in over 200 magazines in Canada, the U.S., Britain, Australia and Italy and have been widely broadcast on television and radio. Di Cicco has also been a seminal figure in Canadian multiculturalism with his edition of *Roman Candles,* an anthology of Italo-Canadian poetry. He lives in Toronto.

Books: *We Are the Light Turning,* 1975
        The Sad Facts, 1977
        The Circular Dark, 1978
        Dancing in the House of Cards, 1978
        A Burning Patience, 1978
        The Tough Romance, 1979
        Dolce Amaro, 1979
        Flying Deeper into the Century, 1982
        A Straw Hat for Everything, 1982
        Dark to Light: Reasons for Humanness, 1983
        Women We Never See Again, 1984

Born in Italy in 1949, MARY DI MICHELE has lived in Canada since 1955. She has worked as poetry editor for *Toronto Life* and *Poetry Toronto* and has edited an anthology of contemporary women poets, *Anything is Possible*. Di Michele won first prize for poetry in the CBC literary competition 1980 and the Silver Medal for the DuMaurier Award for poetry in the National Magazine Awards 1982.

Books: *Tree of August,* 1978
        Bread and Chocolate, 1980
        Mimosa and Other Poems, 1981
        Necessary Sugar, 1984

DON DOMANSKI was born in Sydney, Nova Scotia in 1950, and now lives in Wolfville, N.S. His work has appeared in leading Canadian magazines, on CBC *Anthology,* and on other CBC radio programmes. Recently his work was included in the *Oxford Book of Canadian Verse.*

Books: *The Cape Breton Book of the Dead,* 1975
        Heaven, 1978
        War in an Empty House, 1982

ENDRE FARKAS was born March 11, 1948 in Hajdunanas, Hungary. He left Hungary with his family during the 1956 uprising and moved to Canada, where he has lived in Montreal ever since. He teaches at John Abbott College.

Books: *Szerbusz,* 1974
        Murders in the Welcome Cafe, 1977
        Romantic at Heart & Other Faults, 1979
        Face-Off, 1980
        From Here to Here, 1982

RAYMOND FILIP was born in Lübeck, Germany in 1950. He became a Canadian citizen in 1965 and received his education at McGill University. He lives in Montreal and runs the multicultural reading series Pluriel.

Books: *Jaws in a Fishbowl,* 1976
      Somebody Told Me I Look Like Everyman, 1978
      Hope's Half-Life, 1983

JUDITH FITZGERALD was born in Toronto in 1952. Her criticism, reviews and feature articles have appeared in newspapers and magazines across the country. She has been an editor, journalist, teacher, songwriter and cab driver.

Books: *City Park,* 1972
      Journal Entries, 1975
      Victory, 1975
      Lacerating Heartwood, 1977
      Easy Over, 1981
      Split/Levels, 1983
      The Syntax of Things, 1984
      Beneath the Skin of Paradise, 1984

ARTIE GOLD was born January 15, 1947 in Brockville, Ontario. He was raised in Montreal and continues to live there.

Books: *cityflowers,* 1974
      Mixed Doubles (with Geoff Young), 1975
      Even yr photograph looks afraid of me, 1975
      Some of the cat poems, 1978
      before Romantic Words, 1979

KRISTJANA GUNNARS was born in Iceland in 1948 and emigrated to Canada in 1969. B.A. Oregon, M.A. Saskatchewan, "hopeful Ph.D. Manitoba sometime." She has worked as a freelance translator and as a university instructor and high school teacher. Her poems, stories, articles and translations have appeared in various journals in Canada, Iceland and the United States.

Books: *One-Eyed Moon Maps,* 1980
       Settlement Poems 1, 1980
       Settlement Poems 2, 1980
       Wake-Pick Poems, 1981
       The Axe's Edge, 1983

BRIAN HENDERSON was born in Kitchener, Ontario. Has a Ph.D. from York University. Married and divorced. Presently lives with Brenda, two cats and a school of tetras in Toronto.

Books: *The Expanding Room,* 1977
       Paracelsus, 1977
       The Viridical Book of the Silent Planet, 1978
       Migration of Light, 1983
       The Alphamiricon, 1984

Born and raised in Winnipeg, DIANE KEATING attended the University of Manitoba before moving to Rome, Italy and Montreal. She now lives in Toronto, and most of her poems are written in her Victorian gingerbread house, or in her cottage on the coast of Maine. Her second book, *No Birds or Flowers,* was nominated for the Governor-General's Award in 1982.

Books: *In Dark Places,* 1978
       No Birds or Flowers, 1982

Born in Calgary in 1955, ERIN MOURÉ attended the University of Calgary before moving to Vancouver and briefly attending UBC. She still lives in Vancouver and works for VIA Rail. Her first book of poetry, *Empire, York Street*, was on the short list for the Governor-General's Award in 1979. In 1982 she won the DuMaurier Award for poetry.

Books: *Empire, York Street,* 1979
       The Whisky Vigil, 1981
       Wanted Alive, 1983

KEN NORRIS was born in New York in April 1951 and came to Canada in 1972. He attended SUNY at Stony Brook (B.A.), Concordia University (M.A.), and McGill University (Ph.D.). His work has been published in literary magazines across Canada and the United States. During the 1983-1984 school year, he was writer-in-residence at McGill University.

Books: *Vegetables,* 1975
       Under the Skin, 1976
       Report on the Second Half of the Twentieth Century, 1977
       The Perfect Accident, 1978
       The Book of Fall, 1979
       Autokinesis, 1980
       Eight Odes, 1982
       To Sleep, To Love, 1982
       Acts of the Imagination, 1983
       Whirlwinds, 1983
       The Better Part of Heaven, 1984

MONTY REID was born in Saskatchewan in 1952 and has lived in Alberta since 1968. He has an M.A. in English from the University of Alberta. He currently divides his time between his family in Camrose and his job at the Tyrrell Museum of Palaeontology in Drumheller. He is a founding editor of *The Camrose Review* and editor/publisher of Sidereal Press.

Books: *Karst Means Stone,* 1979
      Fridays, 1979
      The Life of Ryley, 1981
      The Dream of Snowy Owls, 1983

ROBYN SARAH was born in New York in 1949. She grew up in Montreal, where she still lives. Her poems and short stories have been appearing in Canadian quarterlies since 1973. Co-founder (with Fred Louder) of Villeneuve, a Montreal small press, she is currently one of the editors of the serial poetry anthology *Four By Four.*

Books: *Shadowplay,* 1978
      The Space Between Sleep and Waking, 1981
      Three Sestinas, 1984
      Anyone Skating On That Middle Ground (in press)

SHARON THESEN was born October 1, 1946, in Tisdale, Saskatchewan and grew up in small towns in B.C. She went to Vancouver in 1966 to attend Simon Fraser University and has lived in Vancouver ever since. She has published poems, articles and essays on poetry in both Canadian and American journals. She edited Phyllis Webb's *The Vision Tree* (winner of the Governor-General's Award, 1982). Thesen is poetry editor of *The Capilano Review* and teaches English at Capilano College.

Books: *Artemis Hates Romance,* 1980
      Radio New France Radio, 1981
      Holding the Pose, 1983

Other Books in the House of Anansi Poetry Series

Please order from your local bookseller, or write to Anansi for further information.